Colleges & Universities

Educational Spaces

Colleges & Universities

Sibylle Kramer

Educational Spaces

BRAUN

CONTENTS

Colleges & Universities

by Sibylle Kramer

Colleges & Universities – Educational Spaces contains 57 international projects that were completed within the past few years. Even though college and university architecture also often connotes the structure of the various degree programs and curricula, this selection of international projects shows that the concepts and ideas of higher education institutions are converging and similar architectural concepts have become apparent within the past few years. While the term college is still traditionally dominated by British elite institutions such as Oxford and Cambridge, the concept of educational institutions and their architectural requirements has long since been adjusted to the needs of modern education. In terms of content, in Europe, for example, the Bologna process has advanced the creation of a European higher education area, which intends to make academic degree and quality assurance standards more comparable and compatible throughout Europe. The expectations of students towards their educational institutions are evolving accordingly, especially given the increasing number of semesters abroad. In some locations, entire campuses are being restructured while in others only individual buildings are added that have become necessary due to the creation of new academic departments or simply to provide space for modern research institutions. Despite the increasing importance of electronic networking within colleges and among universities, printed materials are not losing any of their significance. Not only Master's and PhD theses, but also professional dissertations and other publications have to be collected and made accessible. The capacities of the old libraries are not sufficient for the flood of new information, which is why an increasing number of new libraries have emerged over the past few years.

High-quality materials and sustainable construction styles are a particular area of concern to allow future generations of students to carry on the educational tradition to the 21st century. The Alma Mater, the nourishing mother who satisfies the hunger for knowledge of students from around the world, is posing new challenges for architects. Numerous departments have long since been added to the original seven liberal arts. Increasingly, specialized knowledge requires specialized buildings to convey it. Thus even highly specialized institutes such as the cloud research laboratory, are housed in appropriate architectural structures. While the purpose of the building is not immediately apparent, its outward appearance immediately reveals to the observer that this is a special type of institution. In addition to multimedia requirements of educational buildings, networking and sustainability of the campus grounds are another focus. Since networking also advances research and teaching, it is very legitimate to reflect this tight network in the façade of buildings, such as the university building in Jussieu.

At the same time, the new architectural projects of universities, colleges and academies enables global storage and access to the continuously growing wealth of information in the form of theses, dissertations, books, and other documents. They offer room and work stations for individual study, as well as seminar buildings and even sports and leisure facilities. Cafeterias with the associated food supply facilities are also included and constitute an additional challenge for architects. Although degree programs are politically matched, the curricula are getting increasingly varied every semester and the variation of educational buildings increases accordingly. Education is the most important issue of the future and architecture provides it with a solid sustainable basis for the next century, as can be vividly seen by the following pages that feature projects from every continent.

Campus

↑ | **Night shot**
→ | **Façade**

Ewha Womans University

Seoul

Flying is the best way to reach the shores of Seoul Ewha University's new building. A landscape then, more than an architecture work, located in the perridst of Seoul's university area. A long asphalted strip, delineated at one end by a race track, and, completely surrounded by nature. Black asphalt, red race track, green nature and finally the white brightness of a valley appears. A valley, which is drawn in the ground, slides down along a gentle slope. At the other end, the slope becomes a huge stairway which can be used as an open air amphitheater if necessary. At the very heart of the valley, a subtle and serene universe appears suddenly. Classrooms and libraries, amphitheaters. Everything follows up with a constant natural light.

PROJECT FACTS

Address: 11–1 Daehyun-Dong, Seodaemun-Gu, Seoul 120–750, South Korea. **Client:** Ewha Campus Center Project T/F, Ewha Womans University. **Partner architects:** Baum Architects, Seoul. **Completion:** 2008. **Size:** 70,000 m².

↖↖ | Exterior view
← | Interior view
↖ | Façade
↑ | Staircase
↙ | Sections
↓ | Floor plan

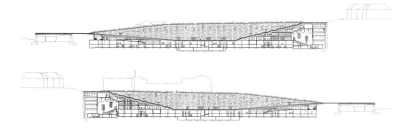

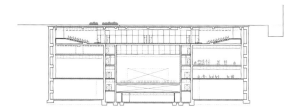

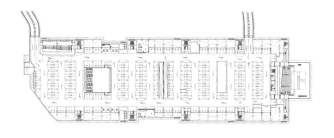

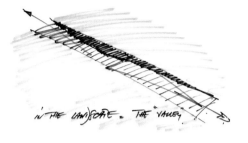

IN THE LANDSCAPE = THE "VALLEY"

←← | Night shot
↙ | Roof garden
← | Interior view
↑ | Sketch
↓ | Huge stairway

↑ | **Exterior view**
→ | **Interior view**

IT University
Copenhagen

The IT University appears open and inviting – forming a frame around students, professors and researchers of the university; a building in spatial dialogue with its surroundings and, at the same time, responding to the city by opening up and letting university activities interact as an asset to the neighboring space. The concept of the design of the university is that of a spatial network – a web in which each function is placed in a three-dimensional position around a central panopticon. The hall at the reception area offers a complete view of the university. From here it appears as a buzzing, spatial structure in which activities on all levels communicate with each other and with the common facilities located at ground level.

PROJECT FACTS

Address: Rued Langgaards Vej 7, 2300 Copenhagen S, Denmark. **Client:** Ministry of Education. **Completion:** 2004. **Size:** 19,000 m².

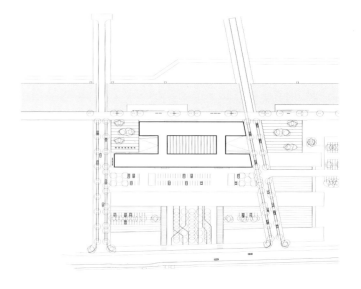

↖ | Exterior view
← | Main entrance
↑ | Site plan
↗ | View by day
→ | Nightshot

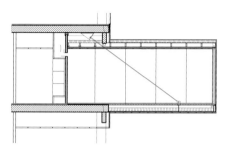

← | **Section box**
↙ | **Section**
↓ | **Interior view,** boxes

↑ | Hall
↓ | Floor plan

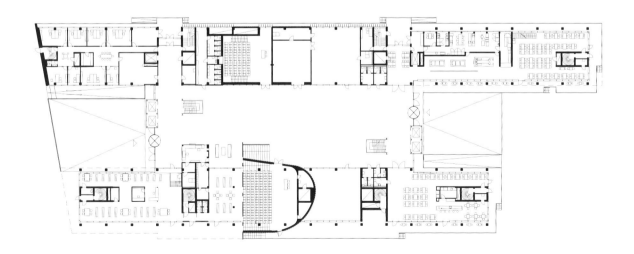

du Besset-Lyon architects

↑ | **Exterior view**
↗ | **Interior view**
↘ | **Lecture hall**

Saint-Denis University
Paris

This project consists of office spaces and educational facilities. The building corresponds to the openness of the site. Its shapes do not impose and the texture of its façades softens its presence. The views slide along the rounded outline of the building and the hierarchy between front and back is challenged. The space turns around the building. Its façades do not assert their presence. Their surface seems to recede and while they blur the repetition and fragmentation effects typical of administrative buildings, they give a perception of the building that is of a global form. The presence of the façades constantly changes following the direction of the sun and the position of the viewer

Address: Université Paris 8, 2, rue de la Liberté, 93526 Saint-Denis cedex, France. **Client:** Paris 8 Saint-Denis University. **Completion:** 2005. **Size:** 6,800 m².

← | Façade
↘ | Floor plan
↓ | Section

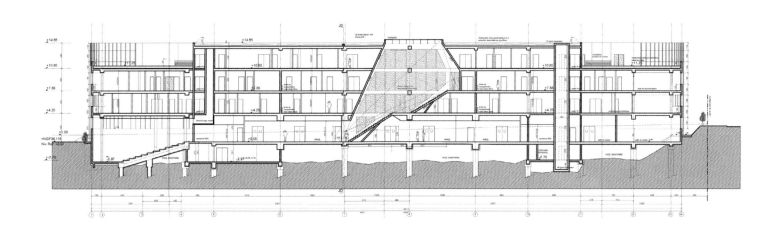

↑ | General view
← | Site plan

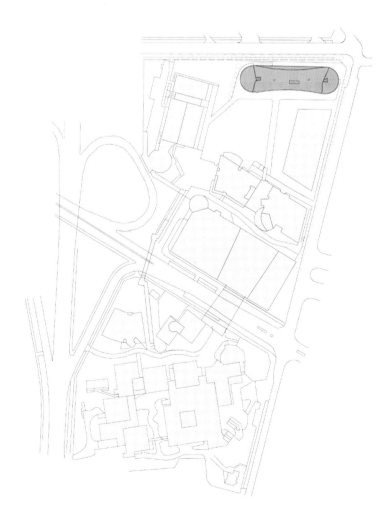

↑ | View from Überseeallee
→ | View from Baakenhafen

HafenCity University

Hamburg

The new construction at HafenCity University, which will serve approximately 1500 students, consists of two sections linked by a hall. Each section has 5–6 floors and a cubic content of approximately 140,000 cubic meters. They feature an underground garage, cafeteria, library, and seminar and study rooms. The foyer and hallways can be used as flexible expansion areas for exhibition, while multifunctional offices offer flexible partitions, and study rooms are available with flexible sizes. The design is distinguished by a great focus on sustainability and energy efficiency, the use of translucent recycling materials for the façades, natural cooling via nighttime ventilation, and the use of thermal storage mass in the ceilings of the individual levels.

PROJECT FACTS **Address:** HafenCity Universität Hamburg, Universität für Baukunst und Metropolenentwicklung, Überseeallee 12, 20457 Hamburg, Germany. **Client:** Freie und Hansestadt Hamburg, Behörde für Stadtentwicklung und Umwelt Hochschulbau-HSB. **Completion:** 2012 (estimated). **Size:** 30,500 m².

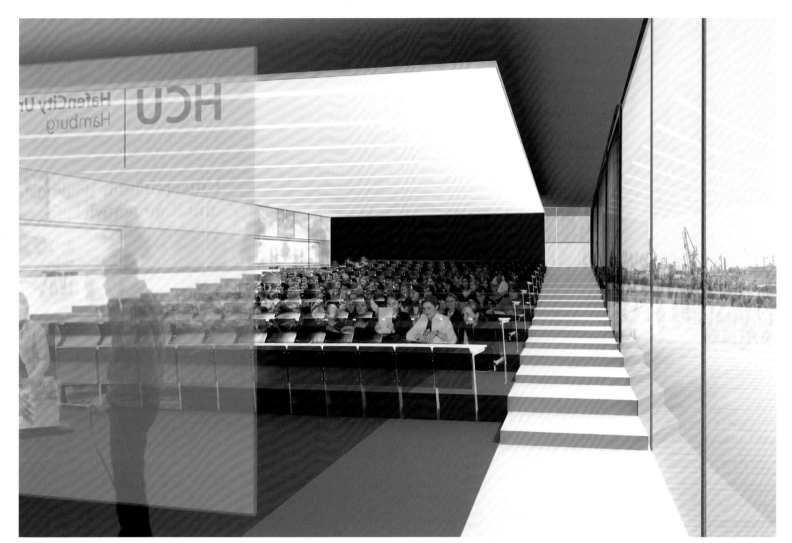

↑ | Lecture hall
↓ | Section

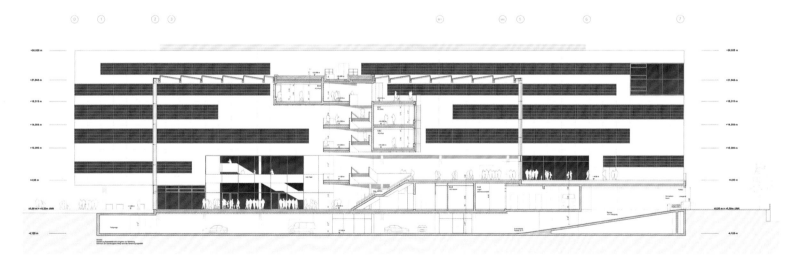

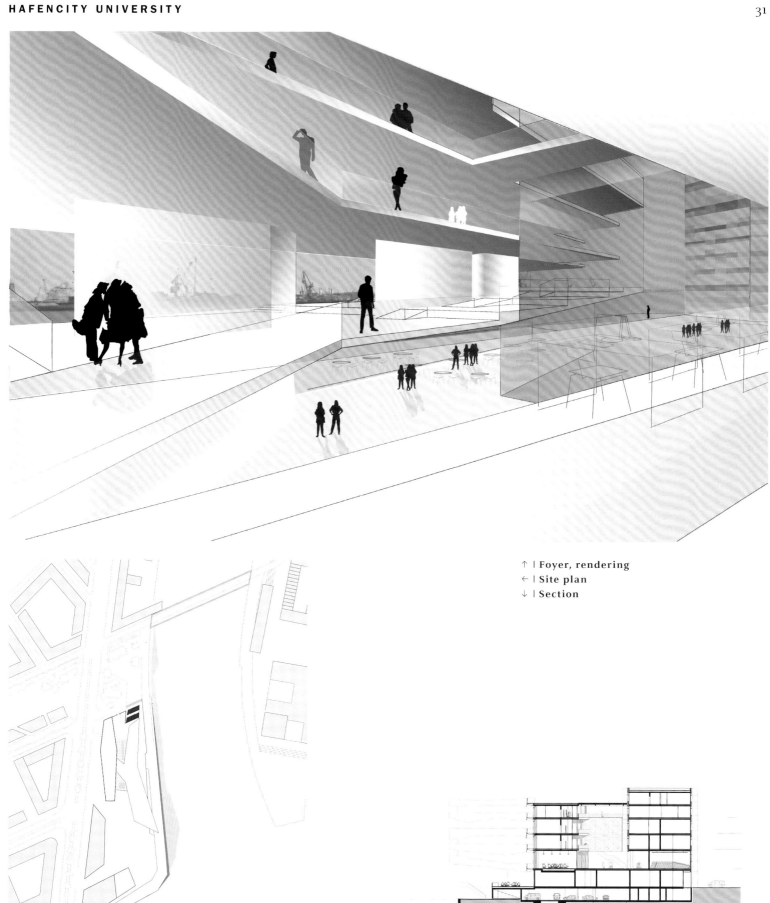

↑ | Foyer, rendering
← | Site plan
↓ | Section

↑ | **Exterior view**
→ | **View to the top**

Atrium Jussieu University

Paris

The 16M building on the Jussieu University campus, near the historic center of Paris, extends and completes the grid plan that architect Edouard Albert designed in the 1960s to serve 45,000 students and researchers. The design of the extension by Périphériques is based on the existing system, in which buildings are laid out in a crown configuration, but at the same it alters it – where Albert laid out a single patio, Périphériques planned two. One of them is covered by bridge-buildings that have been raised to create short-cuts in the circular itinerary forming a "vertical place" that groups all the movements of the buildings. The heaviness and hardness of this concrete space is opposed to the light-weight metal cladding of its outer skin.

PROJECT FACTS

Address: 10, rue Cuvier, 75005 Paris, France. **Client:** Établissement Public du Campus de Jussieu (EPCJ). **Completion:** 2006. **Size:** 16,895 m².

↑ | Meeting point
← | Plan
↓ | Sections
→ | Atrium

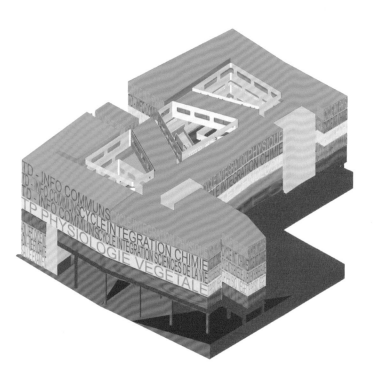

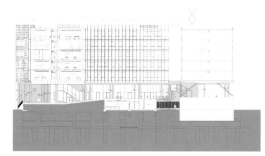

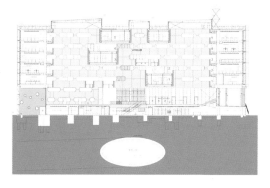

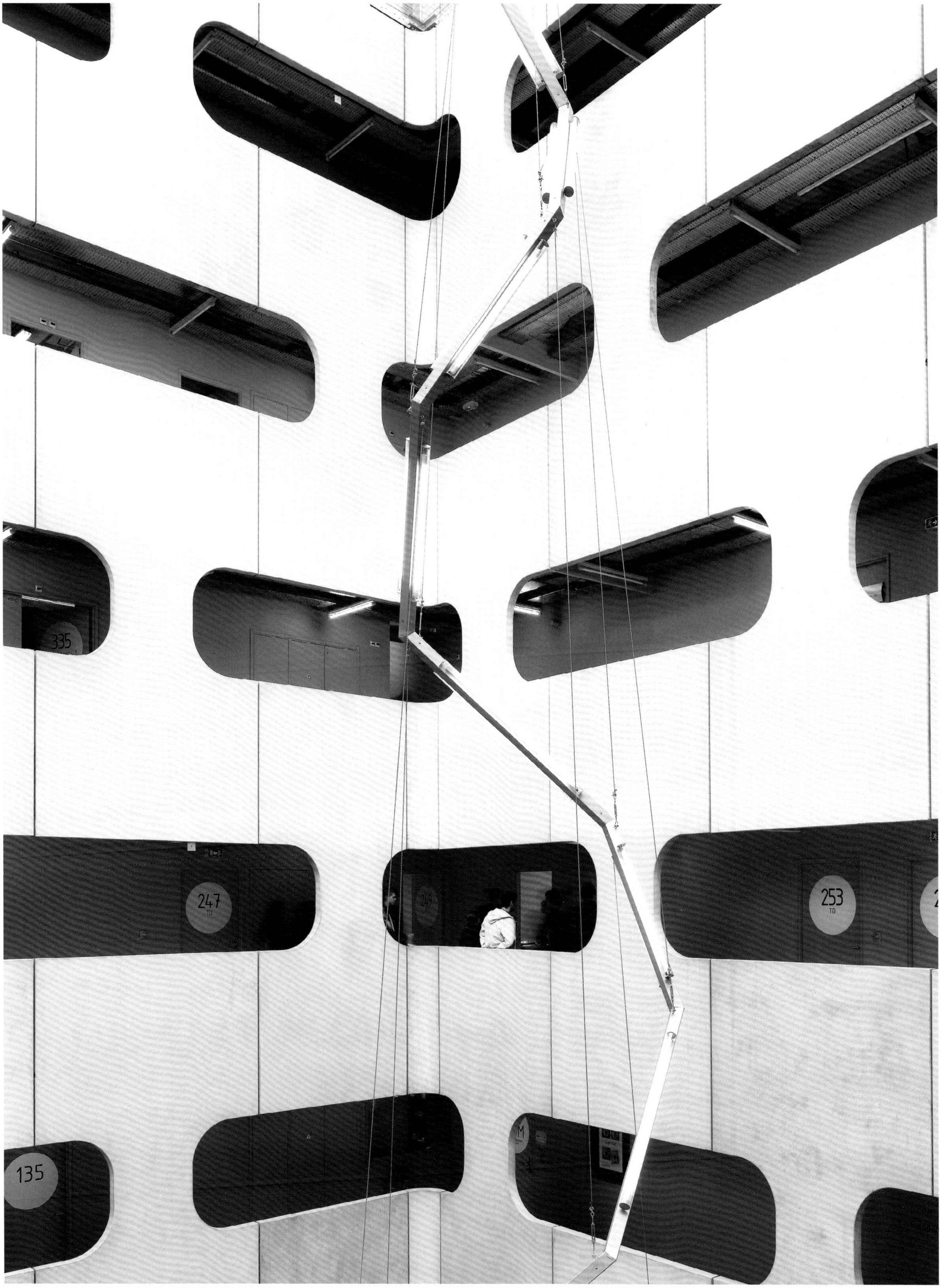
335
247
TD
253
TD
135

↑↗ | **Façade details**   ↓ | **Exterior view**

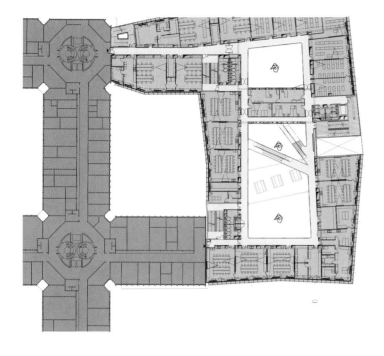

↖ | Floor plan
↑← | Atrium interior view

↑ | **Exterior view**
→ | **Corridor third floor**

DGIT Electron Department

Dongguan

The Dongguan Institute of Technology is a new campus situated on the undulating hills of the Songshan-Lake New Town in Dongguan. The hills are covered with beautiful Litchi trees, while the valleys form natural ponds. Because of its program-determined large size, the Electrical Engineering Department building adopts a horizontal posture parallel to the elongated contours, juxtaposing with the undulating hills. This brings the two distinctive forms into sharp contrast. Along the slope, several passages and stairways cut through the building and recreate the experience of climbing up the existing hill. While walking inside the building along the corridors, the alternating open spaces give way to the scenic views of the surrounding. The natural scenery of the northern hill filters into the building through glass panels on either side of the penetrated space, thus establishing a special relationship between the building and the landscape.

PROJECT FACTS **Address:** Dongguan Institute of Technology, Dongguan Songshanhu Guangdong, China. **Client:** Dongguan Institute of Technology. **Other creatives involved:** China academy of urban planning&design. **Completion:** 2004. **Size:** 20,860 m².

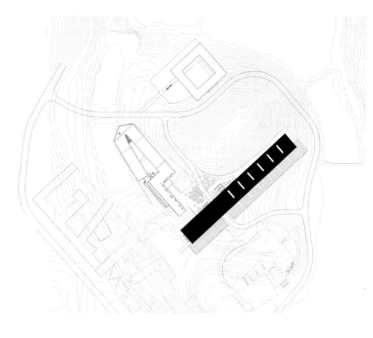

← | Cross space
↑ | Site plan
↙ | South aisle
↓ | Floor plans
→ | East-south elevation

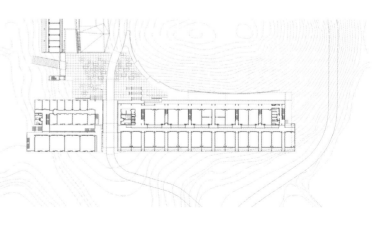

↑ | **Exterior view**
→ | **Inner court**

DGIT Computer Department
Dongguan

The Computer Science Department building is placed along the gentle slopes of the valley and oriented perpendicular to the Electrical Engineering Department building. In order to receive enough daylight, the slopes around the building are partially cut and sustained by retaining walls. The single-sided corridors on the first two floors are open to the internal courtyard, while the corridors on the third and fourth floors are facing towards outside. The long and short corridors facing the outside, meet at the north end, with the best view to the highest and best-preserved hill of the entire campus. The corridors are like two streets leading to a plaza, or the two wings of a boat meeting at the foredeck. A straight flight of stairs connects the internal courtyard with the northern terrace on the third floor, thus tying together the inside and outside corridors.

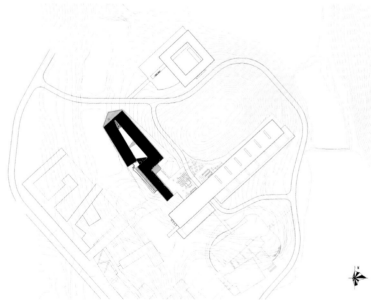

↖↑← | Inner court
↑ | Site plan
↗ | Floor plan
→ | Entrance

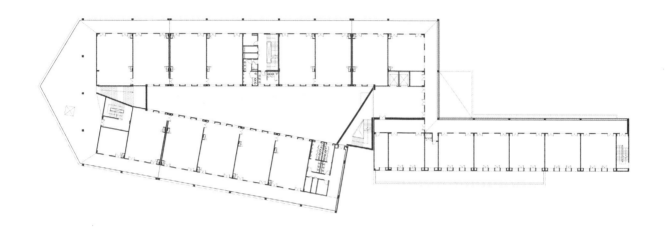

↑ | **Exterior view**
→ | **Façade,** detail

DGIT Liberal Arts Department
Dongguan

The first floor of the Liberal Arts Department building is partly buried into the terrain and merges into the landscape. Because of grade changes, two sides of the first floor remain open and enjoy the nice views towards the nearby pond. The rest of the first floor receives sunlight through an L-shaped internal courtyard. The roof of the first floor creates an open terrace among the undulating topography, while the square upper floors are elevated above the terrace. The combination of courtyard, arcade and terrace create a focused public open space. In the direction of the main circulation, the building mass is broken down and the pressure on the surroundings asserted by the building is relieved. When people look beyond the elevated building and see the rising slopes in the distance, they might be able to imagine or remember how the original landscape looked like.

PROJECT FACTS **Address:** Dongguan Institute of Technology, Dongguan Songshanhu Guangdong, China. **Client:** Dongguan Institute of Technology. **Other creatives involved:** China academy of urban planning&design. **Completion:** 2004. **Size:** 9,150 m².

↑ | Exterior view
↙ | Floor plan
↓ | Site plan
↗→ | Inner court

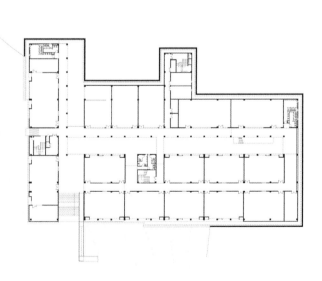

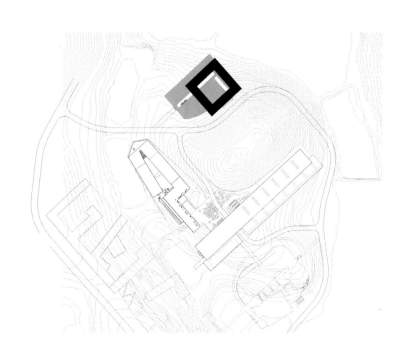

Erick van Egeraat

↑ | **General view**
→ | **Night shot**

INHolland University

Rotterdam

In order to accommodate the rapid growth of INHolland University in Rotterdam, 15,000 square meters hosting study areas, classrooms, commercial functions and offices were added to the original building from 2001. The extension was delivered in 2008 and consists of three interconnected parts. A lower, three-level building is situated parallel to and connecting with the original building. It supports one end of a nine-level bridge building that spans 35 meters over the courtyard and underlying Metro line and rests on a student apartment building at the other end. Finally a higher volume partially cantilevered from the bridge building, offers panoramic views towards the harbor. The façades of each building volume differ, while their architectural language relates to the original INHolland University building to form a coherent ensemble.

PROJECT FACTS

Address: Posthumalaan 90, 3072 AG Rotterdam, The Netherlands. **Client:** Hogeschool INHolland.
Completion: 2008. **Size:** 15,000 m².

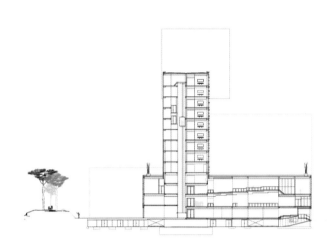

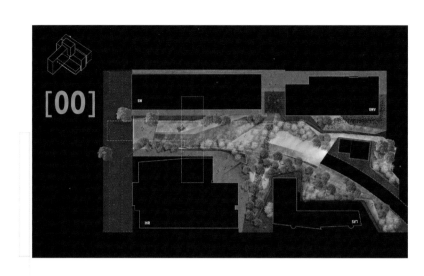

↖ | Section
↑ | Site plan
↙ | Section
↓ | Floor plan
↗ | On the waterfront
→ | Interior view

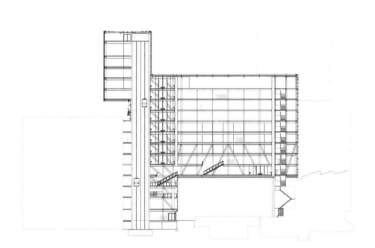

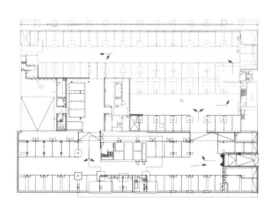

↑ | Aerial view

↓ | Sections
→ | Aerial view

School of Art and Art History

Iowa City

Engaging the edges of the reclaimed pond, the building's edges create new campus spaces, pathways and connections: a campus porosity. To the west, a double height reading room marks a new campus gateway and bracketed between the elevated arms, a sunny desk suspended over the water forms a gathering space. To the north, a serene urban wall of channel glass is set against open campus space. On Riverside Drive, situated in relation to a major path from the main campus, the building's principal entrance occurs under the curving overhand of an auditorium. Internally, this path continues as a public route. Through the multiple access points, campus is drawn into the building. The spaces are low, engaging the pond.

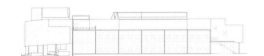

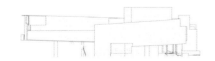

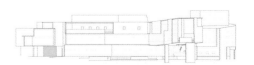

Address: University of Iowa, School of Art and Art History, 141 N. Riverside Drive, Iowa City, IA 52242, United States of America. **Client:** University of Iowa. **Completion:** 2006. **Size:** 6,503 m².

Saucier + Perrotte architectes

↑ | **South façade**
→ | **The Link**

CCT Building

Mississauga

CCT (Communication, Culture and Technology) assumes the role of an interface, closely bordered by a park on one side and a garden courtyard on the other. At ground level is a linear public space linking the other major campus buildings. The plane of the earth forms a continuous public room that slips through the transparent membrane into the building, flows toward the courtyard, onto the landscaped garage roof, and into the campus beyond. Nestled into this landscape are conceptually "mineral" public functions (Multi-Media Studio Theater, the E-Gallery and the Image Bar), each with its own identity but tied together by the new terrain. Strands of topography lift to weave through the upper levels, connecting spaces between the shifting program elements that puncture the façade.

PROJECT FACTS **Address:** CCT Building, University of Toronto at Mississauga, 3359 Mississauga Rd. N., Mississauga, ON L5L 1C6, Canada. **Client:** University of Toronto at Mississauga. **Completion:** 2004. **Size:** 10,800 m².

← | Entrance foyer
↘ | Section
↙ | Site plan
↓ | Floor plan
→ | Entrance auditorium
↘ | North façade

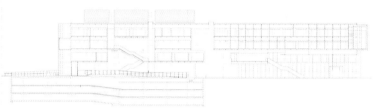

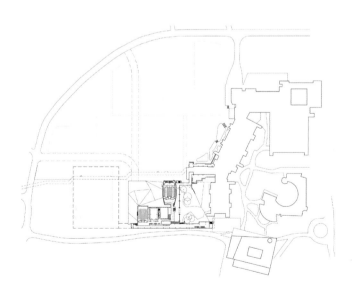

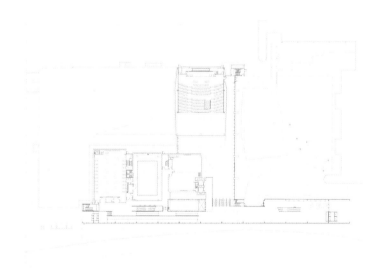

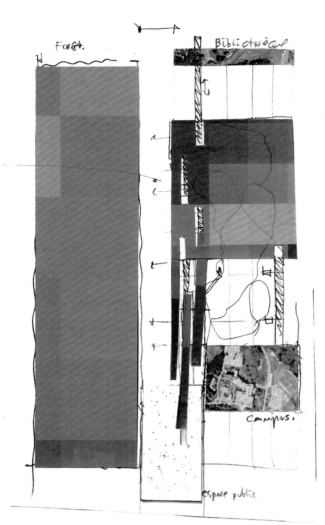

← | Sketch
↓ | Model
→ | South façade
↘ | Entrance foyer

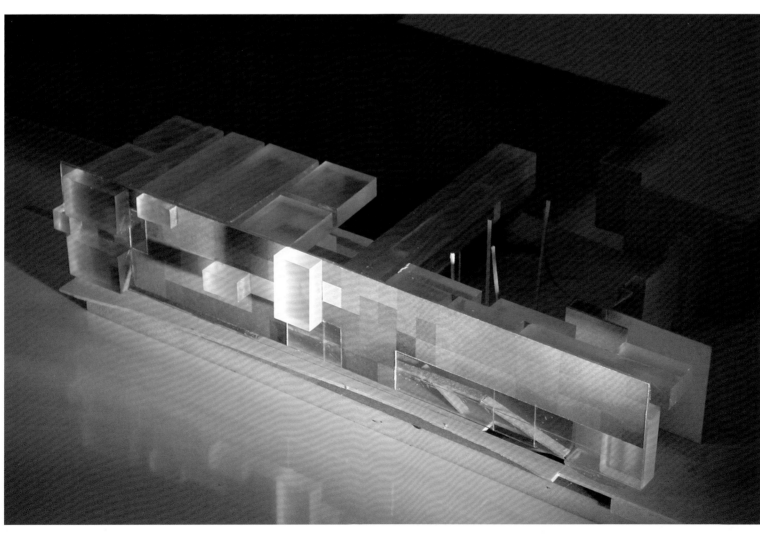

Dietmar Feichtinger
Architectes

↑ | **Exterior view**
→ | **Interior view**

Danube University

Krems

The building program for the new campus includes the erection of a new university of applied sciences, a film gallery with a study center, an auditorium, a library as well as numerous other facilities for the existing and rapidly expanding Danube University. The location on a slope between the voluminous old building and a romantic estate of villas among the vineyards presented the challenge of connecting extremely heterogeneous contexts. Instead of making parallel wings the architects decided to build a comb-like structure. Three parallel, broadly projecting volumes at the upper edge of the site produce a situation that, in contrast to an underground ambiance, creates even in its low-lying internal courtyards a free, open and transparent ensemble of coolly self-assured educational buildings.

PROJECT FACTS

Address: Dr. Karl Dorrekstraße 30, 3500 Krems, Austria. **Client:** Favia Grundstückvermietungsgesell-schaft mbH, State Niederösterreich. **Completion:** 2005. **Size:** 16,675 m².

←← | Interior view
↙ | Aerial view
← | Connection
↓ | Floor plans

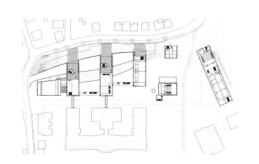

← | **Exterior view**
↓ | **Sections**

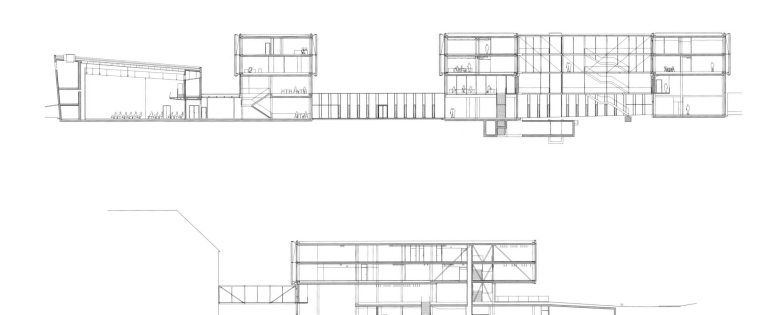

↑ | Façade
↓ | Sections

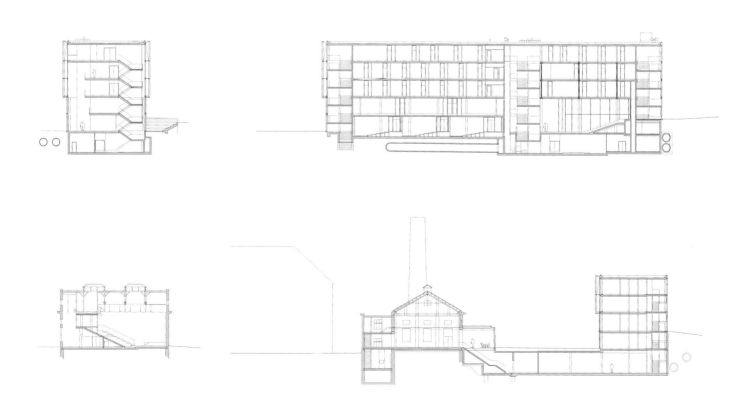

↑ I **Sports hall**
→ I **View from courtyard**

Vigo University Campus

Vigo

Due to the nature of each department it was necessary to redefine the qualities of the entire location and determine how to project them in the future. The architect proposed to work in two apparently opposing directions that will allow an appreciation of the two already existing qualities. Firstly, to emphasize the natural features of the setting, a magnificent location with small inland valleys and exceptional topography. For this purpose, a new access ring road, car parks, extensions to each department, integrated services, reforestation, and a global proposal for the waste water collector were introduced. Students were allowed to make use of the landscape, which offers an ideal setting for silence, concentration, and intense personal work. Secondly, on a more short-time scale, the new constructions redefined the community nature of university life.

PROJECT FACTS

Address: Campus Universitario, C.P. 36310 Vigo (Pontevedra), Spain. **Client:** Ciudad Universitaria de Vigo S.A., Universidad de Vigo. **Completion:** 2003. **Size:** 60,000 m².

← ← | General view
↙ ↙ | Exterior view
← | Lecture room
↙ | Site plan
↓ | Floor plan
↓ ↓ | Sections

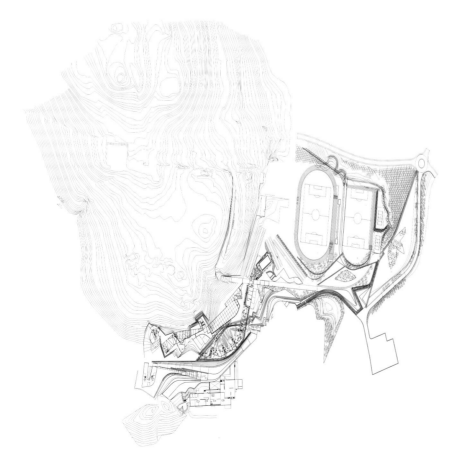

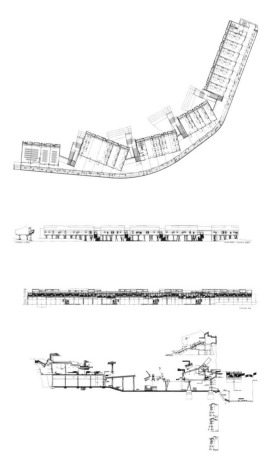

↑ | **General view**
→ | **Exterior view**

Campus Plateau

Daejeon

Due to the lack of plain quarters, the site of the university was made by extensive cuts to a sloped hill. The project's name "culture center" implies that it is a facility for students to congregate for social and cultural activities. The given program for the space speaks for its multiplicity – multi-purpose theater, rooms for clubs, restaurant, conference rooms, exhibition space, counseling quarter, and language lab were all required. The functions of these spaces are too diverse and independent to be grouped under one roof. Of course certain functions need close relationships but controlling these various functions through one entrance was unnecessary if not impossible, and it was advisable to allow different events to be simultaneously held in various places. Moreover, the idea of housing free-willed students within the confined space of an inadequate interior seemed to be ill-conceived.

PROJECT FACTS
Address: Hyehwa Culture Center for Daejeon University, 96–3 Yongun-dong, Dong-gu, Daejeon, Korea.
Client: Daejeon University. **Completion:** 2003. **Size:** 103,218 m².

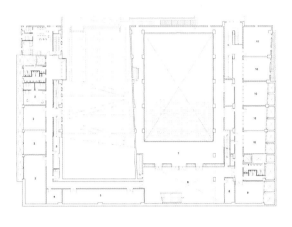

↖↖ | Steps
←← | Exterior view
↖ | Site plan
↗ | Floor plan
← | Courtyard
↓ | Sections

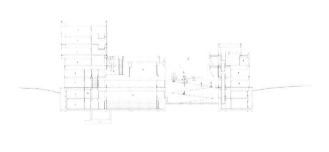

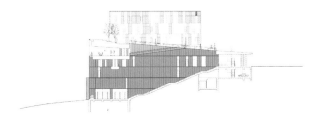

↑↗ | **Exterior view**
→ | **Model**

7th of October University

Bani Walid

Merging the university's art and design faculties, the building's serpentine form bends and curves to reflect the shape of the site, aligning primarily with the base of the Metropolitan Catholic Cathedral. The sculptural form is emphasised by the splayed walls of the studios which provide shade from direct sunlight while maximising natural light from the north. Spanning three stories this entrance draws students, staff and visitors into the central atrium, the social heart of the building. The 11,000 square meters of floor space is distributed over six floors. The lower ground and ground floors provide shared facilities, including the Tate café, seminar rooms, a 350-seat multi-purpose space, galleries and exhibition spaces.

Address: 7th of October University at Bani Walid, Libya. **Client:** Organisation for Administrative Centers. **Completion:** 2012 (estimated). **Size:** 110,000 m².

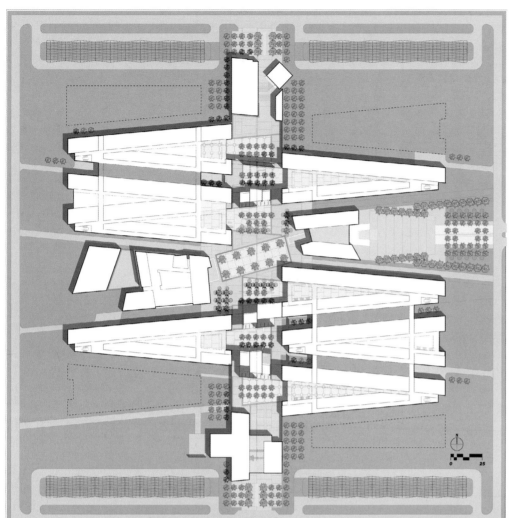

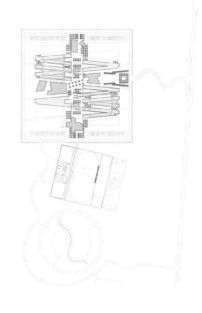

↖↑ | Site plans
↓ | Desert campus
→ | Library
↘ | View of campus

Arkitektfirmaet
C. F. Møller A/S

↑ | **Exterior view**
→ | **Aerial view**

University of Aarhus
Aarhus

The university buildings have grown up around a distinctive moraine gully, where the
individual institutes "wander" on the slopes from the site of the main building on the Ring
Road to the center of the city. The buildings are unique in terms of a continuous university
campus, by virtue of their architecture, the material homogeneity of the façades in yellow
brick, and their adaptation to the landscape. The buildings have become well-known and
recognized, one of the reasons being that the university park now forms an integral set
of buildings that combines a number of the best points of modernism with good Danish
tradition in its design and materials. The university is a unique case of long-term design,
a valuable example of ageless functionalism. Throughout 80 years the university has kept
growing with very different programs, but with the same strict, sober architectonic idiom.

Address: University of Aarhus, Nordre Ringgade 1, 8000 Aarhus C, Denmark. **Client:** Universitets- og Bygningsstyrelsen. **Completion:** 1931–2010. **Size:** 225,000 m².

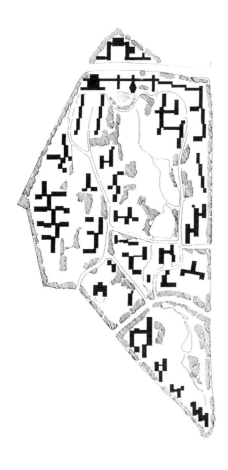

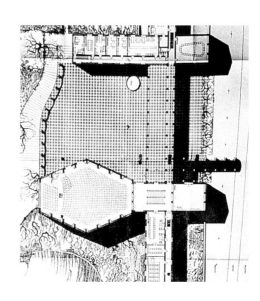

← ← | Main hall
↖ | Site plan
↑ | Floor plan
↓ | Aerial view

Arkitektfirmaet
C. F. Møller A/S

↑ | **Exterior view**
→ | **Lecture hall**

Auditorium Building

Aarhus

A building on this site had to strive to maintain the university's distinct association with the gully and the lakes, so that it is on the one hand a characteristic architectonic element, but on the other hand also fits in with, and is subordinate to, the landscape and the building structure of the university. The auditorium building is in architectonic dialogue with the main building at the other end of the moraine gully. These two buildings contain the more outreaching functions of the university – the main building with its hall and lobby, and the auditorium building with its combination of a lecture and conference complex.

PROJECT FACTS **Address:** University of Aarhus, Auditorium Building, Bartholins Allé, Aarhus Universitetpark, 8000 Aarhus C, Denmark. **Client:** Universitets- og Bygningsstyrelsen. **Completion:** 2001. **Size:** 3,400 m².

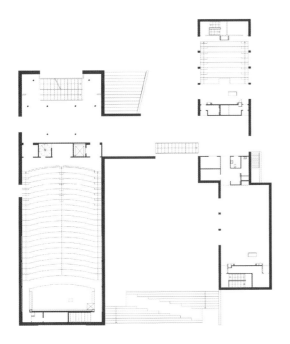

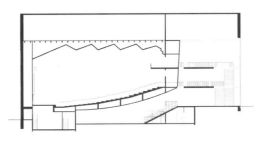

←← | Façade detail
↙ | Interior view
↖ | Floor plan
↑ | Section
↓ | Students' square

↑ | **Construction site**
→ | **Visualisation**

Leipzig University
Main building and auditorium, Leipzig

The design for the new building for the University of Leipzig is situated on the site of the former Pauliner Church. This fourth building section of the university redevelopment consists of three main elements: the auditorium, the main building and the Audimax. The aula with vestry, a contemporary interpretation of the former University Church, is a multifunctional space and will be used – like the original church – for church services as well as for academic ceremonies, concerts and scientific conferences. The main building hosts the university's representative areas, art collection, institute facilities and administrative functions. The building ensemble enables the reintegration of the university campus into Leipzig's city fabric. The university will represent itself with a new and strong appearance at Leipzig's heart, the Augustusplatz, whilst respecting the existing city structure and making reference to the history of the site.

PROJECT FACTS **Address:** Augustusplatz, Leipzig, Germany. **Client:** Free State of Saxony, represented by Staatsbetrieb Sächsisches Immobilien- und Baumanagement Niederlassung Leipzig II. **Completion:** 2011 (estimated). **Size:** 23,936 m².

←← | Interior view
↙↙ | Construction site
↖ | 3D site plan
↑ | Sketch
↓ | Construction site

↑ | **Exterior view**
→ | **View from Boelelaan**

OZW, Vrije Universiteit

Amsterdam

The OZW Health Care and Wellness Education Institute is a new landmark in the architectural landscape of the VU University. It embodies an innovative education concept that combines intermediate and higher level vocational training courses with university courses. Reminiscent of the Amsterdam School, the softly shaped brick walls match the nature of the training programs. The positioning of the windows emphasizes the verticality and main outlines of the exterior and immediately draws attention to the transparency and vitality of the interior: a playful combination of training centers situated around atria. From the south, the atria gradually and diagonally provide access to the facilities. Long lines of sight reduce the size of the building. From the base, for instance, one can see all the way up to the sixth floor. The training institute provides a playful landscape for roaming, seeing and meeting others.

PROJECT FACTS

Address: De Boelelaan 1105, 1081 HV Amsterdam, The Netherlands. **Client:** Vrije Universiteit Amsterdam. **Artist of the artwork on the lecture hall:** Morgan O'Hara. **Completion:** 2006. **Size:** 20,250 m².

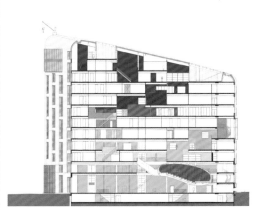

↖ | Lecture hall
↑↑ | Sketch
↑ | Section
← | Hanging lecture hall
↓ | Floor plans
↗ | Picnic tables outside
→ | Computer center

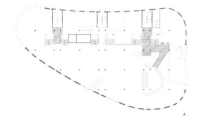

Ferdinand Heide

↑ | Exterior view
→ | Axis Campus Westend

Campus Westend of Goethe-Universität

Frankfurt am Main

Based on the design concept for the upgrade of the Campus Westend, all departments will be situated in a park-like campus. At its heart, the campus contains a stretch of extensions to the existing Hans Poelzig buildings, which contain the central services. The new departmental buildings are positioned along the edge, constituting a curb to the city. In addition to his overall and outdoor premises plans, in the first construction stage, Ferdinand Heide planned the lecture hall building and the cafeteria. Both buildings present themselves as similarly shaped structures positioned across from each other near the new university to square. Their architecture is based on a central theme: they conceptually respond to Poelzig's architecture with an individual contemporary interpretation.

Address: Campus Westend Frankfurt, Grüneburgplatz 1, 60323 Frankfurt am Main, Germany. **Client:** Goethe-Universität, Frankfurt am Main, Hessisches Baumanagement. **Landscape architects:** ARGE Topos Berlin / Ferdinand Heide architect. **Completion:** 2008. **Size:** 12,000 m² (lecture hall center), 4,205 m² (extension Casino) and 34 ha (masterplan).

↑ | Lecture hall
↓ | Sections

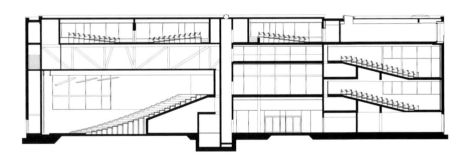

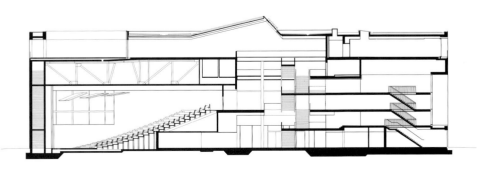

↖ | Staircase
↗ | Foyer
↙ | Floor plans

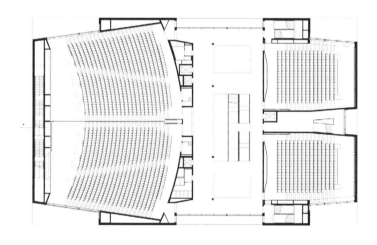

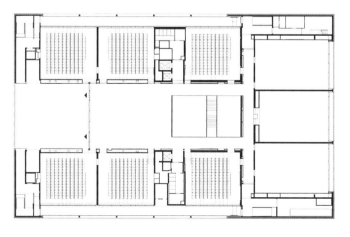

↖↖ | Aerial view
←← | Refectory
↑ | Extension Casino
↙ | Floor plan

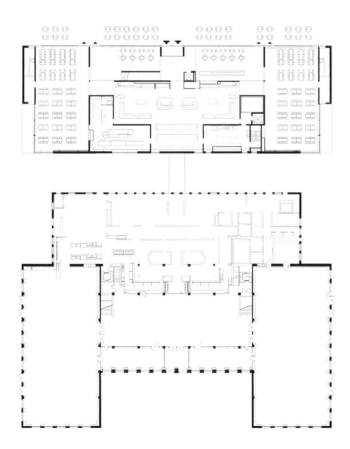

schmidt hammer lassen
architects

↑ | 3D illustration
→ | Construction site

City of Westminster College

London

The college's exceptional new campus in central London will provide state-of-the-art facilities for students as well as a superb amenity for the local community. Designed to be open, connected, flexible and inspiring, it has a simple geometric form that rotates around a dynamic, spiralling inner atrium. Teaching facilities include specialist workshops, laboratories and studios, a large sports hall, as well as classrooms, with flexible study areas in and around the atrium. In addition, there is a theater, café and other public areas. The building takes full advantage of adjoining urban green spaces. Cantilevered decks to the south create solar shading while external green roofs and terracing form an integral part of the design. The campus will be sustainable and energy efficient, with low life cycle costs and maintenance liabilities.

PROJECT FACTS

Address: City of Westminster College, 25 Paddington Green, London W2 1NB, United Kingdom.
Client: City of Westminster College. **Structural engineering:** Buro Happold. **Completion:** 2010.
Size: 24,000 m².

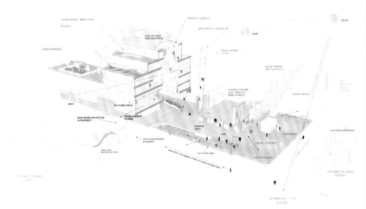

↖↙ | 3D illustration
↑ | Sustainability diagram
↗→ | Construction site

↑ | **Night shot**
→ | **Façade**

Newcastle College
Newcastle upon Tyne

RMJM has designed five major projects at Newcastle College's Rye Hill Campus. The series of new projects are seen as playing a major role in regenerating the campus and surrounding community. The award winning new buildings include the Performance Academy which combines the Music, Performing Arts and Media; SPACE a reconfiguration of the existing 1960's concert hall to provide a Higher Education Center with bar, café, exhibition and conference space; refurbishment of grade B listed Ryehill House provides student support and administration facilities; the Lifestyle Academy combines food, hospitality, beauty, travel, customer services, sport departments, with the facilities being open to the public; and lastly the Sixth Form College.

Address: Newcastle College, Rye Hill Campus, Scotswood Road, Newcastle Upon Tyne NE47SA, United Kingdom. **Client:** Newcastle College. **Completion:** 2010. **Size:** 35,000 m².

↑ | Ryehill house
↙ | Sketch

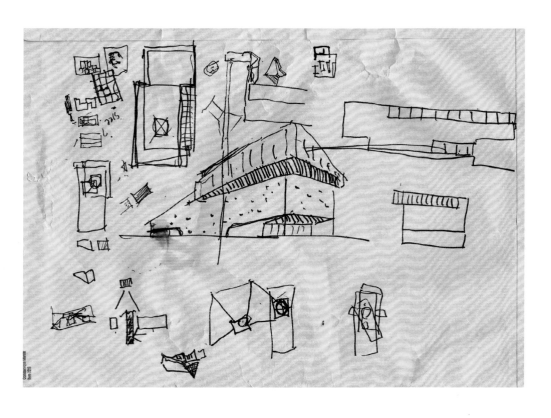

↑ | Visualisation
↙ | 3D site plan

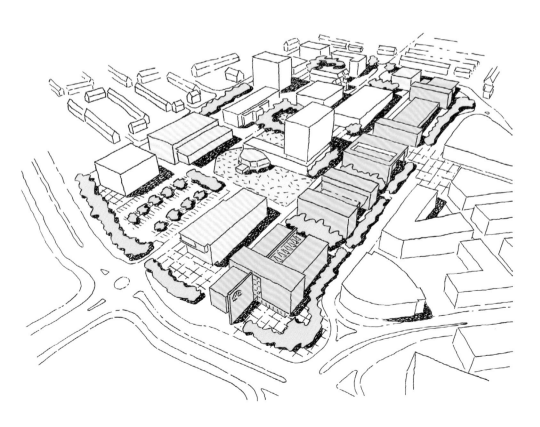

↑ | **Interior view**
→ | **Exterior view**

Senior Common Room

Oxford

This sensitive project extends the existing senior common room building, which dates from 1676 and is Grade 1 listed. The design provides new sitting rooms, a roof terrace and an extended lunch room on the first floor. The first floor dining area cantilevers into the garden and is wrapped in a two-story, free-standing glass box. Weathered oak louvres sit outside the box on a flitched steel and oak frame and are set against a backdrop of nearby tree canopies. The extension is more a garden pavilion than a building extension, allowing the natural surroundings of the garden to reach into the building, rather than the building encroaching upon it. From inside, the dialogue with the gardens has a contemplative quality. Within the existing building, rooms are remodelled and disabled access improved.

PROJECT FACTS
Address: St John's College, Oxford OX1 3JP, United Kingdom. **Client:** St John's College, Oxford.
Completion: 2004. **Size:** 90 m².

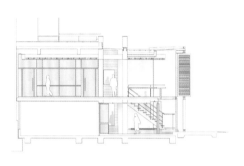

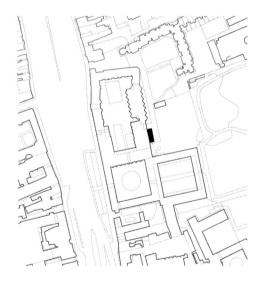

↖ | Dining room
↑↑ | Section
← | Staircase
↑ | Site plan
↗↗ | Floor plans
→ | Sitting room

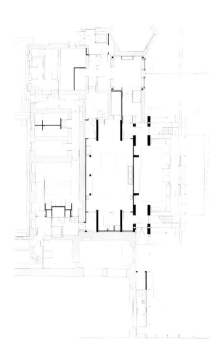

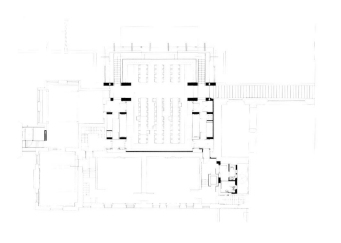

↑ | **Exterior view**
→ | **Entry to Center for Wellness**

Center for Wellness

New Rochelle

The Center for Wellness at the College of New Rochelle is designed as an abstract representation of a paradisiacal garden. The Center merges building and landscape into a physical, intellectual and spiritual experience, through the use of natural materials and light. The natatorium is a grotto carved beneath a contemplation roof garden. Skylights allow daylight to the surface of the pool water below. The gymnasium emerges from the topography like a rock outcropping with its locally quarried granite walls. The lobby concourse is a crevasse cut deeply into the sloping site and connects the gym to the pool.

PROJECT FACTS

Address: 215 Liberty Street, New Rochelle, NY 10805–2338, United States of America. **Client:** The College of New Rochelle. **Completion:** 2008. **Size:** 5,100 m².

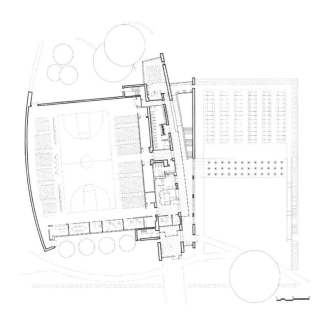

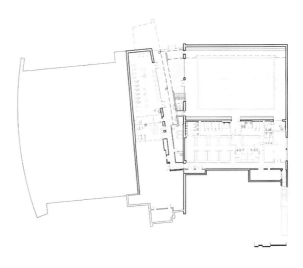

↖↖ | Roof garden
↙↙ | Natatorium
↖ | Floor plans
↓ | Holistic meditation

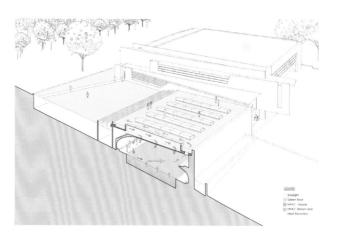

← | Sketch of Crevesse
↑ | Sustainability diagram
↓ | Exterior view of Holistic Meditation Room
↗ | Concourse west
↘ | Concourse east

↑ | External view
→ | Internal atrium

Bournville College

Birmingham

Bournville College is home to some 15,000 learners and has been at its current location for over forty years. The growth of student numbers at the college alongside the deterioration of its premises meant a new home was a necessity rather than a luxury. The timing for the opportunity of a new landmark building which would attract new learners in a state-of-the-art environment was fortuitously coupled with the redevelopment of Longbridge in South Birmingham. The new 64 hectare masterplan meant that not only would the college directly influence the lives of learners, but by being at the heart of the new community, it could indirectly affect the lives of all the community.

PROJECT FACTS

Address: Longbridge Lane, Northfield, Birmingham B31 2TW, United Kingdom. **Client:** Bournville College. **Completion:** 2011 (estimated). **Size:** 23,500 m².

↑ | Exterior view

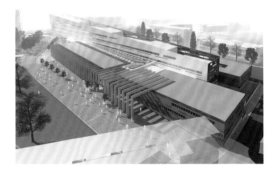

↑ | Renderings
↓ | Main entrance

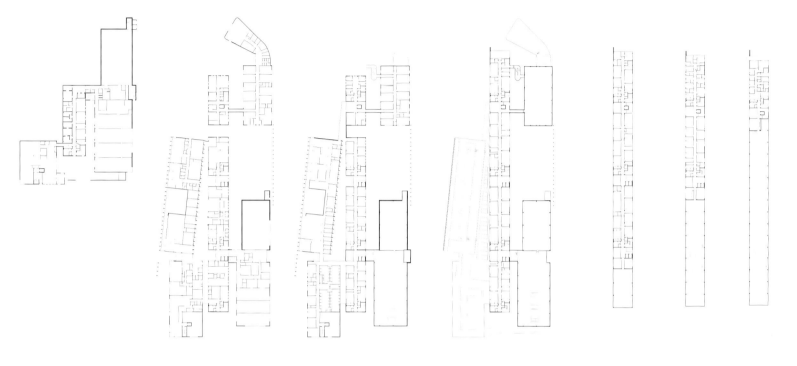

↑ | Floor plans -1 to 5
↓ | Night view

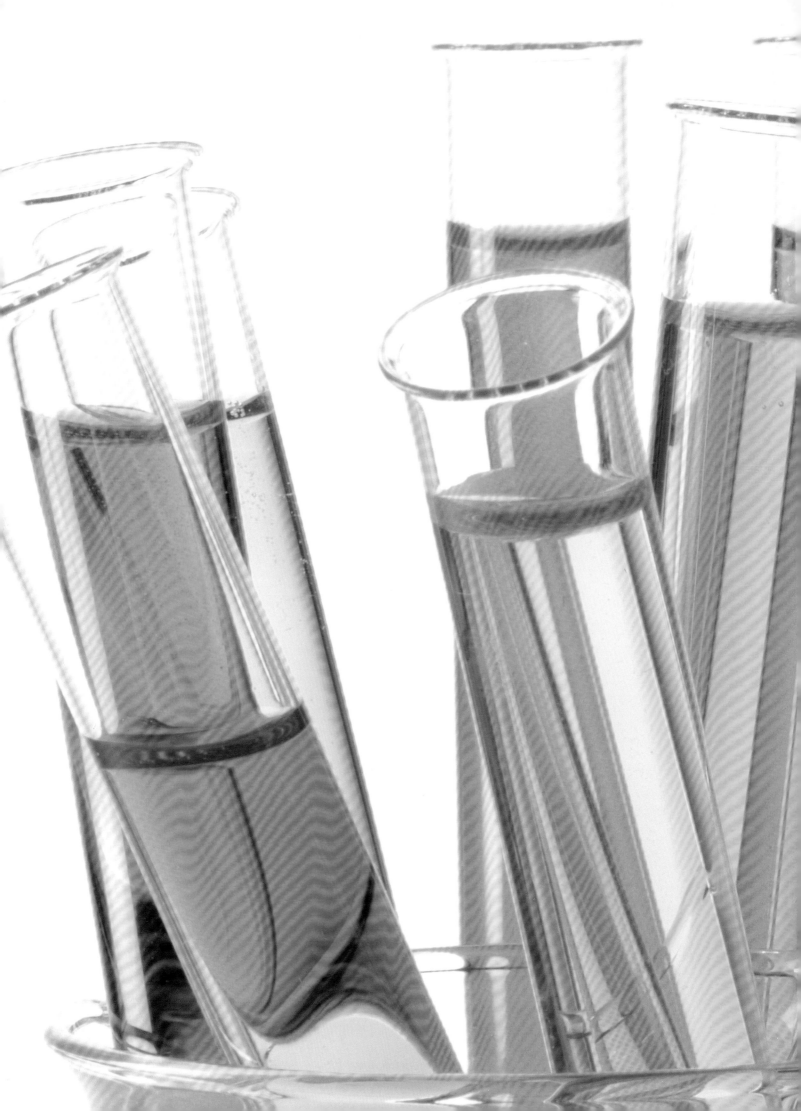

Research

Jarmund/Vigsnæs
AS Architects MNAL

↑ | **Exterior view**
→ | **Façade**

Svalbard Science Center

Spitzbergen

The new structure is an addition to an existing university and research building, which was expanded to about four times its original size. The project also provides new facilities for the Svalbard Museum. The insulated copper-clad skin is wrapped around the structure, creating an outer shell to accommodate the flows of wind and snow passing through the site. Climatic 3D simulations were carried out to ensure that snow would not accumulate excessively in front of doors and windows. The building is elevated on poles to prevent the melting of the permanent frost – the only solid foundation of the construction. The main structure is made of timber to facilitate on-site adjustments and avoid cold bridges. The outer copper cladding retains its workability even at low temperatures, thereby extending the construction period further into the cold season.

PROJECT FACTS

Address: Longyearbyen, Svalbard, Spitzbergen, 78° north, Norway. **Client:** Statsbygg / Norwegian Directorate of Public Construction and Property. **Completion:** 2005. **Size:** 8,500 m².

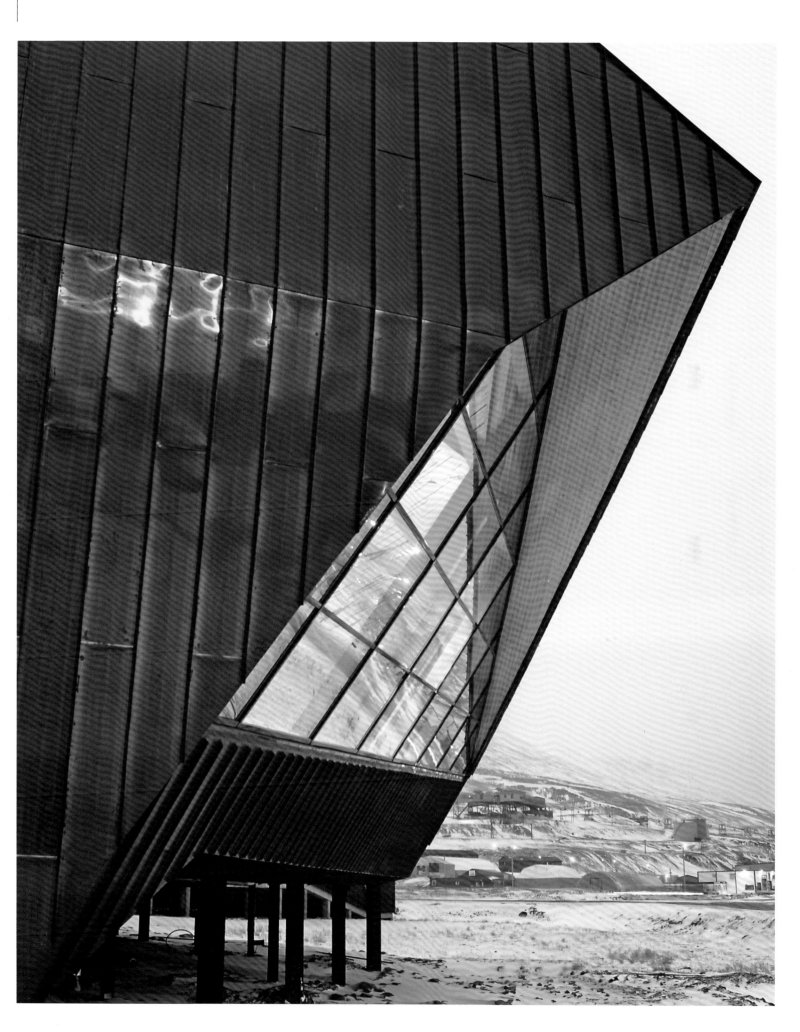

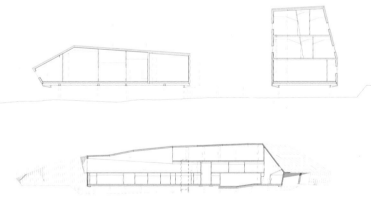

↑↑ | General view
← | Exterior view
↑ | Sections
↗ | Window
→ | Interior view

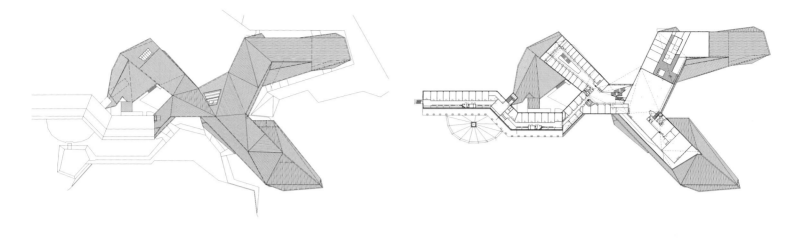

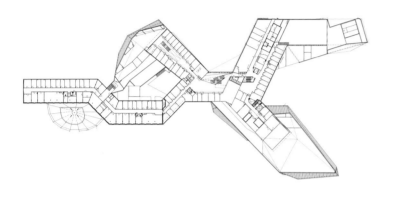

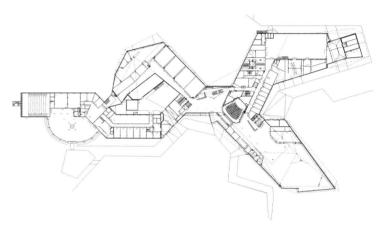

↑ | **Floor plans**
↓ | **Panorama**

↗ | **Corridor**
↗↗ | **Staircase**
→ | **Interior view**
→→| **Overlys**

↑ | **Exterior view**
→ | **Balcony**

Cloud Laboratory

Leipzig

The architectural shape is not derived from the emotional concept of clouds, such as a "cloudy" building or an amorphous shape. Instead, the cloud laboratory is the visual expression of highly technical machinery which focuses on controlling clouds in test tubes. The uniqueness of the experiments conducted with the cloud simulator lends the building a particular appearance. The peripheral laboratories and offices are arranged at a single level around the 16-meter tower of the cloud simulator. Similar to this symbolic typology of the building, the individual design elements are also derived from the world of cloud research.

PROJECT FACTS

Address: Leibniz Institute for Tropospheric Research, Permoser Straße 15, 04318 Leipzig, Germany.
Client: Leibniz Institute for Tropospheric Research e.V., Prof. Dr. Jost Heintzenberg. **Completion:** 2005.
Size: 1,353 m².

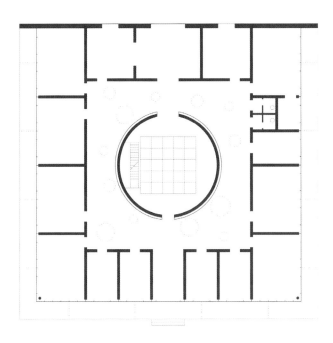

← | Tower interior
↙ | Areaway
↑ | Floor plan
→ | Interior view
↓ | Site plan, section

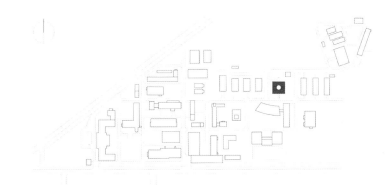

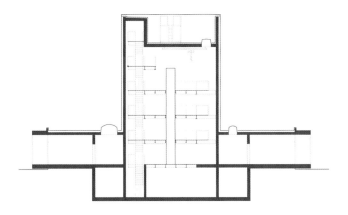

↑ | **View of hub**
→ | **Primary arrival view**

School of Medical Research

Sydney

This new school provides an integrated medical teaching and research environment based on the contemporary educational principles of student centered learning and collaborative research. The key design idea was to create a "socio-educational" external hub space, joining with and extending the vocabulary of the other spaces throughout the campus. This external room provides a focal point for the three different programs (teaching labs, office accommodation and research laboratories) to collaborate within the medicine discipline. The strong visual and spatial interconnection of the curved link which forms the external room blurs the program's delineation, mixing researcher, educator and students.

PROJECT FACTS **Address:** Goldsmith Avenue, Campbelltown, NSW 2560, Australia. **Client:** University of Western Sydney. **Completion:** 2008. **Size:** 8,120 m².

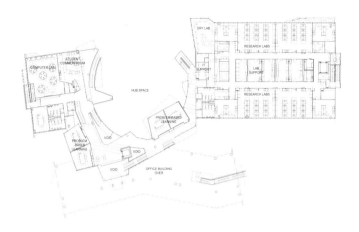

↖ | Floor plan, level 1
↑ | Site plan
← | Floor plan, level 2
↓ | Student collonade
↗ | View out
↘ | View into hub

↑ | **Exterior view**
→ | **Interior view**

UEL Clinical Education Center

London

This building offers three main functions – a 24-seat podiatry clinic and associated bio-mechanical laboratories, five sub-divisible physiotherapy studios, and a sports science laboratory. The positioning of the building encloses the campus to the east and spans the former "The Green" road extending east to west. The podiatry section is situated to the north and the physiotherapy and sports science are on the top floor with its own roof terrace to the south. Internally, the plan focuses on a spine corridor in the southern section flanked on both sides by the physiotherapy studios. The specialized biomechanical rooms are located on the top floor of the northern half. The two lower podiatry floors have quite an innovative design as patient privacy is a high priority and at the same time each of the four groups of six students needs to be supervised by a tutor.

PROJECT FACTS

Address: University of East London, Stratford Campus, Romford Road, London E15 4LZ, United Kingdom. **Client:** University of East London. **Completion:** 2006. **Size:** 2,670 m².

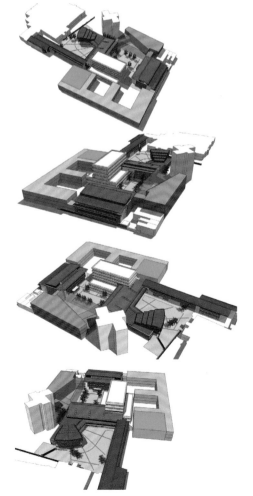

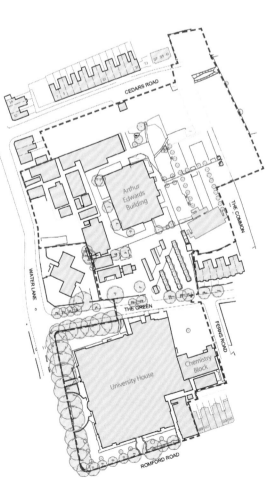

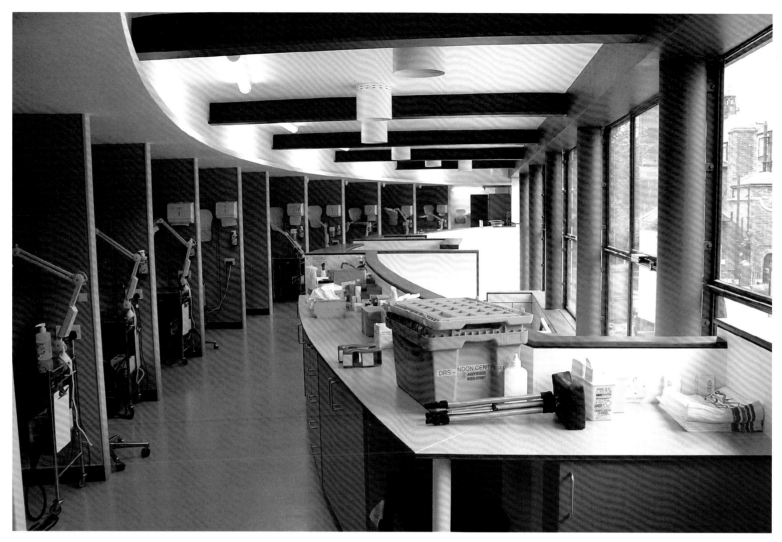

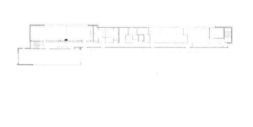

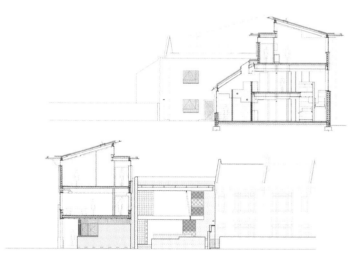

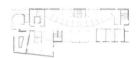

↖↖ | Interior view
←← | Campus site plans
↑ | Podiatry teaching area
↖ | Floor plans 1–3
↗ | Sections

Joachim Kleine Allekotte
Architekten

↑ | **View from south**
→ | **Interior view**

Meridian Buildings

Potsdam

With the renovation of the Meridian buildings, the revamping of the AIP campus has been nearly completed. Identical from the outside, they buildings are individual monuments as well as part of the "Prussian Arcadia" world heritage site. With the support of the European Regional Development Fund, the buildings were renovated and given a new function. The most conspicuous structural change to the architially very neglected but intact Meridian buildings was the new connection building between them. This new wing was implemented as a massive construction of 35 centimeters thick, white lightweight concrete. The aluminum lamellas that constitute the external sunscreen create a formal connection to the wooden cladding of the Meridian buildings. Originally conceived as cold rooms, the buildings were provided with heat insulation in the course of their restructuring.

PROJECT FACTS
Address: Exhibition and media center with a focus on Robotics in the Meridian buildings, An der Sternwarte 16, 14482 Potsdam, Germany. **Client:** Astrophysical Institute Potsdam. **Completion:** 2004. **Size:** 666 m².

← | Entrance
↑ | View from east
↙ | Site plans
↓ | Section

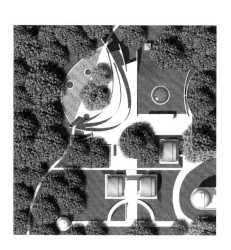

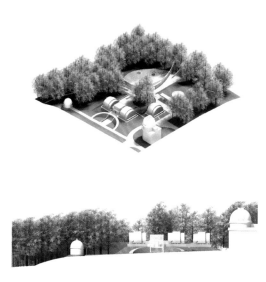

↑ | **Exterior view**
→ | **Interior view**

Model Animal Research Center
Nanjing

Model Animal Research Center of Nanjing University, situated in the high-tech zone in Pukou, Nanjing, is composed of three parts, the office and lab building, the power center and the mouse-breeding lab. Office and lab building focus on the discipline among various parts of utilization as well as the internal and external relationship. The relationship between courtyards and buildings is somewhat similar to that between traditional Chinese gardens and cities as the background of these gardens. With the lab facing the west, the office and the mouse room is in south and north respectively. According to different appearance due to the utilization and strict geometric connection, these three parts constitute a harmonious entity. The six staircases are linked with the corridor in the two stories high space, connecting all parts of the entire building, hence creating more opportunities for researchers to meet with one another. Many successful cases have proved that a lot of discoveries in scientific research come exactly from those accidental and informal exchanges.

PROJECT FACTS
Address: West to Xuefu Road, Pukou High-tech Zone, Nanjing 210093, P.R. China. **Client:** Model Animal Research Center of NJU. **Completion:** 2003. **Size:** 5,500 m².

↑ | **East façade**
← | **Site plan**

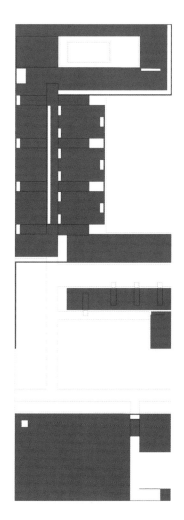

↑ | Entrance side
← | Floor plans

↑ | Night shot
→ | Tall studio

Sackler Building
London

The new Sackler Building provides new purpose made accommodation for all the painting students at the Royal College of Art to work together under one roof for the first time in over 10 years. The Sackler Building is the first phase of the RCA's plan for a major new campus in Battersea, also designed by Haworth Tompkins. The second phase will start on site in January 2010. The Sackler Building was always conceived as a conversion; the old building – a single story factory – has been transformed into a series of new day lit spaces under a dramatic new roof form, by inserting a new independent steel structure within the existing brick enclosure. This has significantly increased the height of the building, providing several double height studios along with a mezzanine level, which houses a number of smaller top lit studios, whilst retaining a predominantly open plan environment.

PROJECT FACTS

Address: 14-22 Howie Street, Battersea, London SW11 4AY, United Kingdom. **Client:** The Royal College of Art. **Completion:** 2009. **Size:** 1,280 m².

← | **Entrance**
↓ | **North lit studios**

↑ | Profiled studio roof
← | Studio
↓ | Site plan

Ernst Giselbrecht + Partner
architektur zt gmbh

↑ | Lecture room
→ | Façade detail

Biokatalyse TU Graz

Graz

The basic urban planning concept of the project was to implement a new architectural arrangement of the surrounding buildings and the premises. This architectural and urban planning design concept is supported by the landscape planning. The building was designed to showcase its laboratory function. The open entrance areas, together with the ground floor, functionally and architecturally interact with the existing biochemistry and chemistry buildings. The colors and structure of the perforated aluminum folding elements positioned in front create a dynamic façade element symbolizing the continuously new positioning of current research. The fluctuation nature of the façade surfaces and their vivid colors are continued inside the building.

Address: Petersgasse 14a, 8010 Graz, Austria. **Client:** BIG BundesImmobilien GmbH. **Completion:** 2004.
Size: 4,400 m².

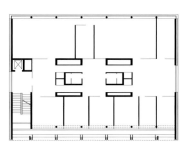

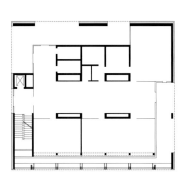

← | Façade, detail
↑ | Floor plans
↙ | Folding elements
↓ | Energy concept sketch
↗ | Façade, open
↘ | Façade, closed

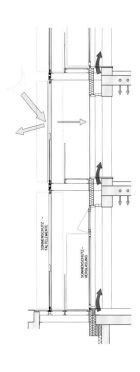

← | Office
↑ | Section
↙ | Sanitary box
↓ | Site plan
↗ | Night view

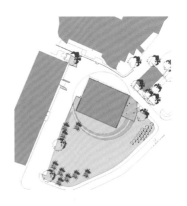

↑ | Exterior view
↗ | Front view
→ | Newsroom

Arizona State University
Phoenix

The Walter Cronkite School of Jounalism and Mass Communication situated in the new LEED Silver 225,000-square-meter building has become an integral part of the fabric of ASU's energizing downtown campus and a pioneering project of Phoenix's redevelopment. Truth and honesty, the guiding principles of journalism and the legendary Walter Cronkite, were the basic concepts of the building's design. The architecture is very expressive in terms of function and materials. The exterior is clad in glass, masonry, and multi-colored metal pancls with patterns inspired by the radio spectrum. The Cronkite School occupies the second and third floors as well as a portion of the fourth and sixth floors of the building. The Cronkite News Watch and KAET Channel 8 Public TV both transmit live from their state-of-the-art studios on the sixth floor.

PROJECT FACTS

Address: 555 North Central Avenue, Phoenix, AZ 85004, United States of America. **Client:** Arizona State University and the City of Phoenix. **Completion:** 2008. **Size:** 2,250 m².

↑ | Broadcast studio
↙ | Floor plans 1–6

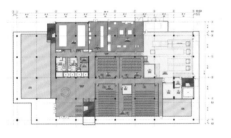  

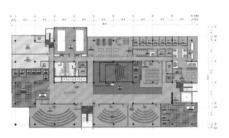 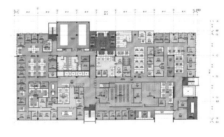

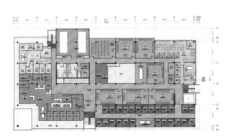 

↑ | **Central forum**
↙ | **Site plan**

↑ | Exterior view
→ | Interior view

TU Darmstadt Extension FB 13
Darmstadt

The extension buildings were added within the context of orthogonal structures of sturdy exposed concrete buildings of the 1970s. In contrast to the extensively subdivided existing cubic buildings, the new buildings are geometrically unambiguous rectangular structures with consistently smooth façades and flush rows of windows. Expanded metal was used as the material for the buildings because of its strong expressive powers. The different times of day, alternating light due to sunshine and clouds, as well as the changing seasons, are all factors that lead to a great variation in the expression of the two structures. Despite the conventional interior layout with central hallways, the color concept and illumination create a variety of settings.

PROJECT FACTS
Address: TUD Lichtwiese, Petersenstraße 12, 64287 Darmstadt, Germany. **Client:** State of Hesse, HBM Süd.
Completion: 2004. **Size:** 5,200 m².

↑ | Interior view
← | Floor plan
↙ | Section

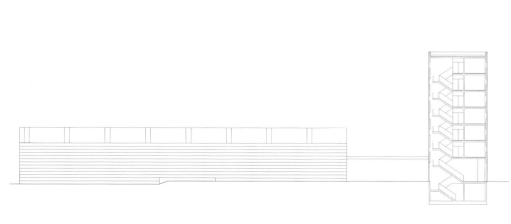

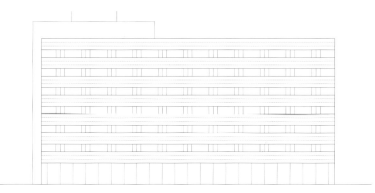

↖ | Façade
↑ | Elevation
↙ | Site plan

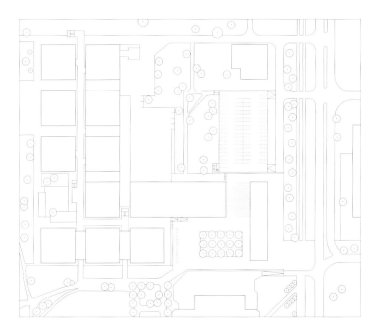

Lecture

Tilman Bock, Norbert Sachs

↑ | **Exterior view**
→ | **Campus site**

Lecture Hall

Zittau

With the addition of various incisions and projections, the originally cubic shape of the building evolved into a structure of great plastic effect in its urban setting. Its structure is determined by the closed volume of the auditorium with the stepped roof terrace above, in addition to the internal layout conceived as a path through the building. Both the roof terrace and the campus square located in front are visible from the foyer. The fusion of external and internal spaces turns the foyer into a central communication area in the new campus layout. Starting from the campus square, the foyer takes visitors to the internal sequence of rooms, passing by lecture halls, and to the upper floor through an extended glass mezzanine level.

Address: Theodor-Körner-Allee 8, 02763 Zittau, Germany. **Client:** SIB Sächsisches Bau- und Immo-bilienmanagement. **Completion:** 2006. **Size:** 2,315 m².

↑ | Façade
← | Floor plans
↓ | Site plan
↗ | Roof terrace
→ | Interior view

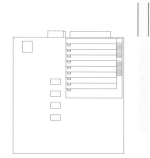

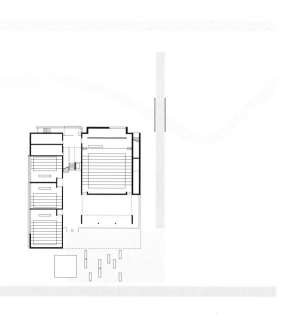

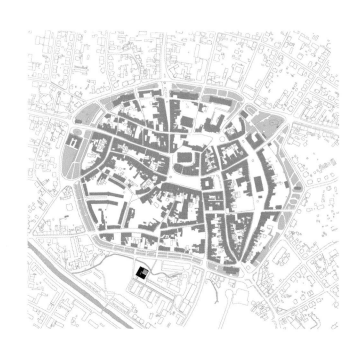

↑ | **Exterior view**
→ | **West façade**

Schulich School of Music
Montreal

Defining the corner of the McGill campus in downtown Montreal, the project connects to the historic Strathcona Building by means of a glass bridge, adding a library, recital hall, offices, and world-class studios to the music faculty. Its five-story multimedia room is anchored three stories into the earth. Evoking an eroded ground leading to Mount Royal, a concrete plane above the foyer and recital hall appears to support the upper volume, including the three-story library. The east façade (clad in zinc) expresses the stratified topos; the west façade (matte and polished aluminum) reflects the historic campus and contains a series of punched windows, evocative of antique piano rolls. The front façade allows daylight to permeate the interior spaces.

PROJECT FACTS
Address: 555 Sherbrooke Street West, Montreal, QB H3A 1E3, Canada. **Client:** McGill University.
Completion: 2005. **Size:** 11,775 m².

←← | Tanna Schulich recital hall
↙↙ | Stairs
← | Exterior view
↓ | Section
↙ | Library
↓↓ | Sketch

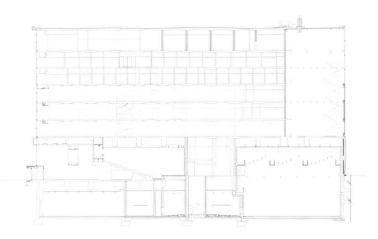

me di um Architekten
Roloff Ruffing und Partner

↑ | **Exterior view**
→ | **Night view**

Central Law Library

Hamburg

The stand-alone building of the new central law library is situated prominently next to the existing law building. Projecting forward into the street alignment, it creates a new fore-court that serves as an entry zone to the campus. However, the main entrance function of the existing law building was retained. From it, the library tower that is enveloped in a glass façade, can be reached through the foyer of the old building. The façade of the cubic library is decorated with multi-colored glass, and thus changes its appearance according to the time of day and season of the year. Linking bridges and stairs cross the atrium, turning this almost ecclesiastical space – five meters wide and 25 meters high – into a true experience. Far below shines the turquoise-colored surface of the water, which serves both atmospheric and air-conditioning purposes. Light conductors mounted beneath the glass roof introduce daylight to the depths of the atrium.

PROJECT FACTS **Address:** Rothenbaumchaussee 33, 20148 Hamburg, Germany. **Client:** Hansestadt Hamburg. **Energy concept:** Transsolar, Stuttgart. **Client:** Hansestadt Hamburg. **Completion:** 2004. **Size:** 6,030 m².

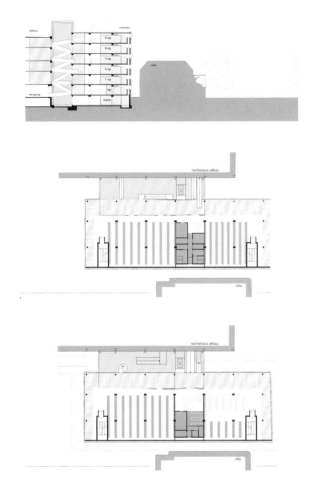

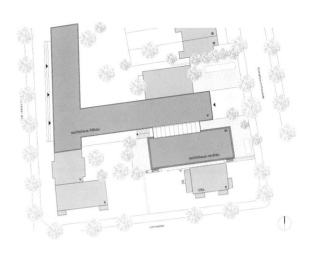

←← | Atrium
↖ | Section
← | Floor plans
↑ | Site plan
↓ | Detail façade

Jean Marc Ibos
Myrto Vitart architects

↑ | **General view**
→ | **Reading room**

André Malraux Library

Strasbourg

The river landscape demands to be understood horizontally. Everything in the setting complies with the logic of the river – the linearity of the quays, the stretch of the jetty, the alignment of the trees. Even the buildings themselves are lined up from one end of the jetty to the other, perfectly regular in their continuity parallel to the quays, vertically punctuated at their ends, like prows, by their silos. On this long tongue of land surrounded by water, it is less the buildings that define the space than the relation between them; the succession of masses and voids, the play of horizontals and verticals, the axes, as well as their strict alignment with the quays.

PROJECT FACTS **Address:** Presqu'Ile André Malraux, 67076 Strasbourg Cedex, France. **Client:** Urban community of Strasbourg. **Signage designer:** Integral Ruedi Baur & Associés. **Completion:** 2008. **Size:** 18,000 m².

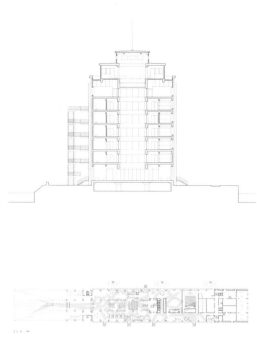

↖ | Detail
↑ | Sections
↗ | Along the docks
→ | Interior view

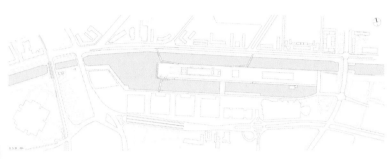

↖ | Ground level
↑ | Site plan
← | Reading room
→ | Layering

... comportait huit chiffres. Elle était ornée d'une petite
... une ancre dessinée à la plume, comme par

La connaissance est à la fois un désir et la découverte
de ce que l'on a cherché. Plotin, Ennéades

↑ | View from the street
→ | Exterior view

Halle aux Farines

Paris

Heavy restructuring was needed to install university facilities in this reinforced concrete market built in 1950. The volumetry of the building was preserved because the envelope structure provides its main strongpoint and architectural niterest. The building has therefore been totally preserved, with its towering ceilings, vaulted reinforced concrete shell and skeleton façades filled with huge prefabricated concrete panels. Only the central bay was entirely emptied to make way for the lecture halls, with no intermediary load-bearing point. These almost back-to-back space, which sit inside the existing envelope like a "ship in a bottle," compose a linear form that is independent of the two side bays and determines an open space beneath the vaulted ceiling in which computer cabins have been installed for the students.

PROJECT FACTS

Address: ZAC Rive Gauche, Paris – 13, France. **Client:** U3M, Rectorat de l'Académie de Paris, Université Paris VII. **Completion:** 2006. **Size:** 17,800 m².

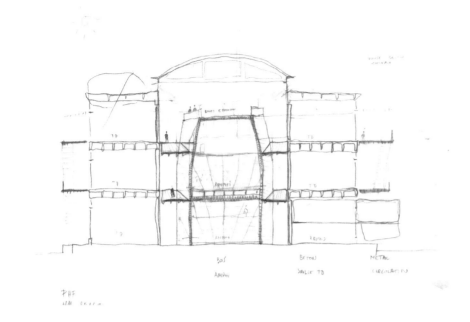

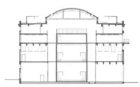

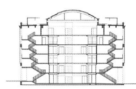

←← | Entrance
↙↙ | Façade by day
↖ | Sketch
↑ | Site plan
← | Sections
↓ | Façade at night

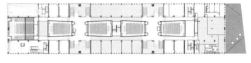

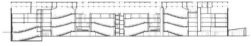

← | Staircase
↑ | Floor plan and section
↓ | Lecture hall
→ | Interior view

↑ | **Rendering**
→ | **Model**

KTH new School of Architecture
Stockholm

Inspired by the concept of a free campus layout that encourages movement, this project aimed to offer new paths and locations. Situated in the most central corner of the campus, the new school of architecture will be a rounded glass and burgundy Corten steel building consisting of six floors, including a sunken garden and a roof terrace. With its curved contour, the school building maintains the nature of the existing courtyard as a single continuous space. At street level, a double height space, containing the work shop, ateliers, and exhibition areas, will constitute the central axis that meanders through the building and provides internal access to the adjacent campus library and campus entrance buildings. The rusted red exterior is compatible with the existing dark red brick buildings of the KTH campus.

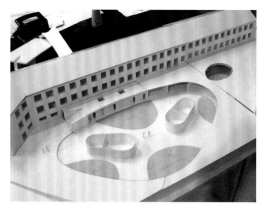
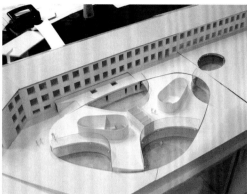
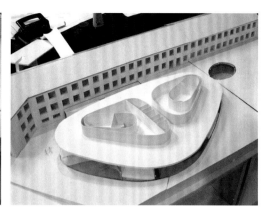

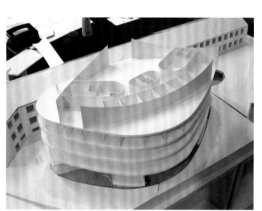

↑ | **Physical model,** ground floor to level 6
↓ | **Floor plans**

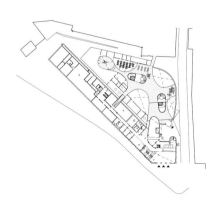
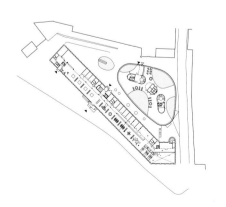

↑ | Rendering
↓ | Floor plans

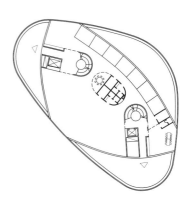

↑ | **Exterior view**
→ | **Interior view**

UEL Cass School of Education
London

The building is organized around a simple idea – everything should be visible on entry and there should be no corridors. A top-lit atrium offers three floors of teaching accommodation on the north side, balanced by four floors of offices to the south. Since the floor to ceiling heights differ on either side, this results in a journey between two stairs on either side from floor to floor to the top. Both offices and teaching rooms are glazed in front so that all the building's activities are clearly visible. There are two "special" features. First, a plywood-clad tower, which cantilevers out into the main space overhanging the entrance desk on the ground floor contains one-to-one interview rooms and an open meeting space at its top. And second, a small music performing room has been placed adjacent to the entrance and implemented as an external object.

PROJECT FACTS
Address: University of East London, Stratford Campus, Romford Road, London E15 4LZ, United Kingdom. **Client:** University of East London. **Completion:** 2009. **Size:** 3,500 m².

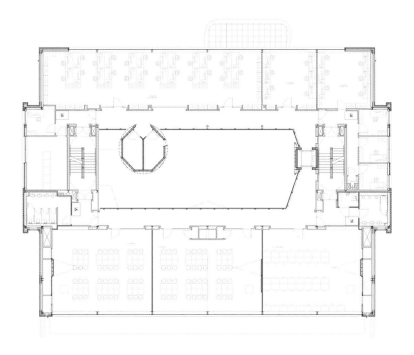

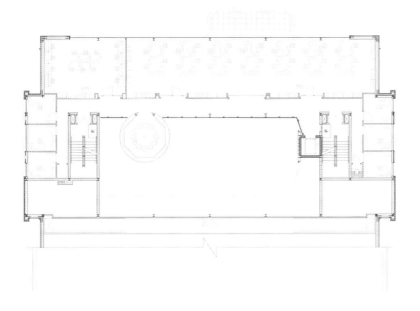

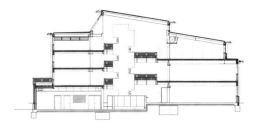

←← | Floor plan, level 2
↙↙ | Atrium interior
← | Floor plan, level 3
↑ | Section
↓ | Classroom interior

↑ | Library
→ | Exterior view

Gateway
Buckinghamshire

Gateway is the centerpiece of the ongoing redevelopment of Buckinghamshire New University's campus in High Wycombe. Located on a constrained and sensitive urban site, the new landmark building accommodates a learning resource center, a multi-purpose sports and events hall, a gym, music and video recording studios, and a drama space. The vision was to create a sustainable and contemporary building that provides facilities for the entire student body and that contrasts with the existing campus architecture to establish a new and distinctive identity for the university. The exciting mix of uses reinforces the public nature of the campus. Providing 24/7 access, it creates a memorable and appropriate "gateway" building for BNU and High Wycombe, consequently raising the expectations and experiences of students, staff and public alike.

PROJECT FACTS **Address:** Buckinghamshire New University, Queen Alexandra Road, High Wycombe, Buckinghamshire HP11 2JZ, United Kingdom. **Client:** Buckinghamshire New University. **Completion:** 2009. **Size:** 10,500 m².

↖ | Central atrium
← | Learning area
↓ | Sketch

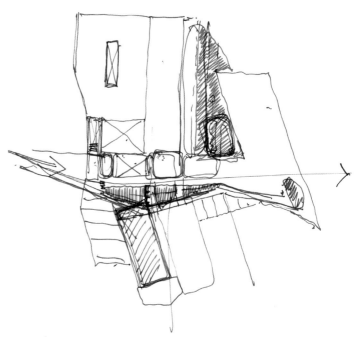

↖ | Sports and events hall
↗ | Detail staircase
← | Learning area
↓ | Floor plans

↑ | External view
→ | Auditorium at dusk

Corpus Christi College Auditorium
Oxford

Rick Mather Architects designed a new flexible multi-purpose performance space for Corpus Christi College in Oxford. Corpus Christi is one of Oxford's oldest colleges founded in 1517. The building site lies in the southwest corner of the college within a bastion of the 13th century city wall. A flexible space was created to accommodate seminars, 136-person lectures, drama, music, a 40-person round-table, banquets for 80 diners and college parties. The new building replaces the existing smaller music room. A skylight above the theater gives views up to Christ Church Cathedral, and a large picture window opposite gives views back to the trees of the college gardens.

PROJECT FACTS **Address:** Merton Street, Oxford OX1 4JF, United Kingdom. **Client:** Corpus Christi College, Oxford. **Completion:** 2009. **Size:** 360 m².

↖ | View across courtyard
↑↑ | Section
↑ | Floor plans 1–3
↗ | Exterior view
→ | Auditorium

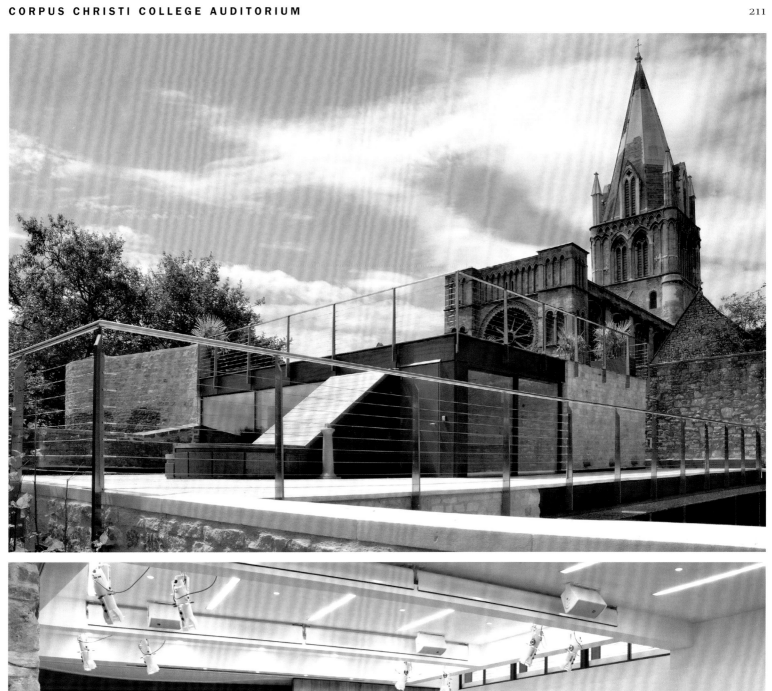

↑ | Lecture hall
→ | Staircase

European School of Management and Technology

Berlin

Constructed from 1962 to 1964 as the official seat of the highest body of the German Democratic Republic, the former State Council Building located at the Schlossplatz square in Berlin, was to be restructured into the "Learning Center" of the ESMT. Due to its original use, the building had high-quality and prestigious interior furnishings. Extensive renovation and restructuring measures were required to adjust the technology and room structure to the needs of a modern university. In close cooperation with the tenant and the Landesdenkmalamt (State department for the preservation of historical monuments) a concept was developed for the key areas crucial to the preservation of monuments. All other rooms were carefully restructured or redesigned.

PROJECT FACTS Address: Schlossplatz 1, 10178 Berlin, Germany. Client: Grundstücksgesellschaft Schlossplatz 1 mbH & Co. KG. Completion: 2006. Size: 18,500 m².

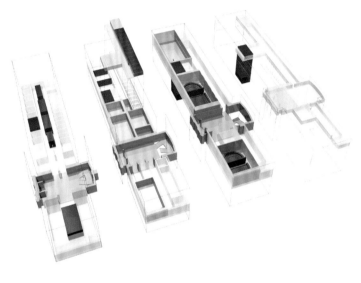

↖ | Competence center
↑ | Floor plans
↙ | Cafeteria
↗ | Foyer
→ | Lecture hall

↑ | Lotus pond
→ | View from CIIE block

Indian Institute of Management
Ahmedabad

The new campus is accommodated in a 39-acre site and includes facilities like nine dormitories for 340 students; an academic block with five classrooms and seminar rooms; administrative facilities; IMDC hostels; 20 blocks for married students; six VIP suites; a sports complex; kitchen and dining facilities; a CIIE block and 100 guestrooms. The public areas are designed to be accessible to the disabled and adequate land has been demarcated for future expansion. Although the new campus functions independently from the old without any direct visual link and even has its own approach road and entrance halls, it is connected to the old campus by means of an underpass (which houses an exhibition on Louis Kahn's work at the old campus). This pedestrian passage is really the pivot and is located such that it not only connects, but really binds the two campuses together.

PROJECT FACTS

Address: Vastrapur, Ahmedabad – 380 015, India. **Client:** Indian Institute of Management, Ahmedabad. **Completion:** 2008. **Size:** 55,000 m².

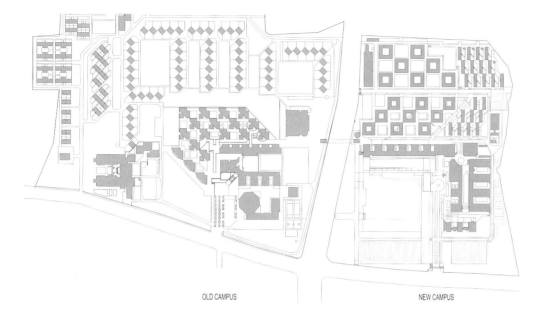

OLD CAMPUS   NEW CAMPUS

↖↖ | Lecture hall
↙ | Courtyard
↖ | Site plan
↓ | Internal courtyard

↑ | **Lobby**
→ | **Stairwell**

NYU Department of Philosophy

New York

A new stair shaft below a new skylight joins the six-level building vertically with a shifting porosity of light and shadow that change seasonally. Prismatic film was installed on
the south-facing stairwell windows which occasionally break the sunlight into a prismatic
rainbow. The ground level, utilized by the entire university, contains a new curvilinear
wooden auditorium on a cork floor. The upper level floors contain faculty offices and
seminar rooms which are done in different shades and textures of black and white, according to the texts in Ludwig Wittgenstein's book "Remarks on Colour".

PROJECT FACTS **Address:** 5 Washington Place, New York, NY 10003, United States of America. **Client:** New York University. **Completion:** 2007. **Size:** 2,787 m².

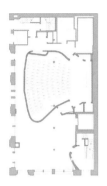
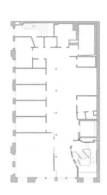
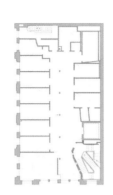
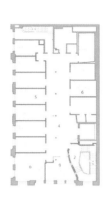
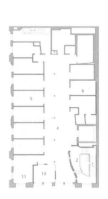
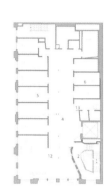

↑ | Floor plans
← | Exterior view
↓ | Section
↗ | Interior view
↘ | Wall panels
↘↘ | Stairs

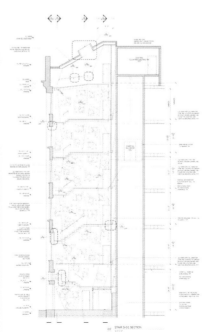

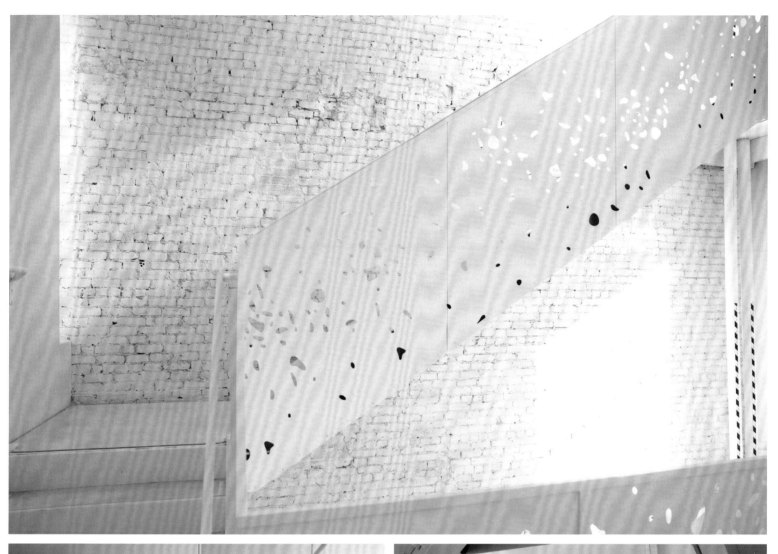

Arkitektfirmaet
C. F. Møller A/S

↑ | **Exterior view**
→ | **Façade detail**

A. P. Møller School

Schleswig

A new Danish co-educational school for the Danish School Association of Southern Schleswig, including students up through the final year of upper secondary school. The school has been designed on the basis of a clear and simple fundamental concept. The building is structured around two large, central spatial elements, one containing common areas with a canteen, reception hall and learning center on three floors, the other main element is a larger sports and multi-purpose hall incorporating three arenas. The school's location and design take a point of departure in the site's interaction with the town of Schleswig and Slien Fjord, as well as in the desire to create timeless architecture.

PROJECT FACTS

Address: Auf der Freiheit, Ilensee, 24837 Schleswig, Germany. **Client:** A. P. Møller and Chastine Mc-Kinney Møller Foundation. **Completion:** 2008. **Size:** 15,000 m².

↑ | Student's lockers
← | Reading area
↓ | Section
↗ | Three levels
→ | Ceremonial hall

↑ | **Front view**
→ | **View from existing building**

University of Cambridge
Department of Architecture, new studio building, Cambridge

The new studio building forms part of a refurbishment and expansion of the Department of Architecture, responding to a brief uniting teaching and research functions. The new studio building sits to the rear of the terrace adjacent to Colin St John Wilson's seminal 1950's extension. Space for the new building was limited: planning constraints meant that existing listed trees needed to be preserved and sufficient space given to the rear of the listed Georgian terrace to preserve its integrity. The placement of the building creates a central cloistered garden space between the new building and the existing extension. The form of the building is determined by its function, and a desire to build a naturally cooled timber-frame building that embodies the department's commitment to sustainable design.

PROJECT FACTS **Address:** 1–5 Scroope Terrace, Cambridge CB2 1PX, United Kingdom. **Client:** University of Cambridge, Department of Architecture. **Refurbishment of existing buildings:** Freeland Rees Roberts. **Completion:** 2007. **Size:** 422 m².

↖ | Façade
← | Aerial view
↓ | Site plan

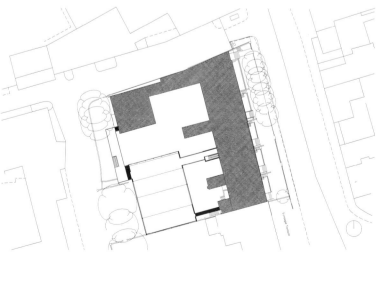

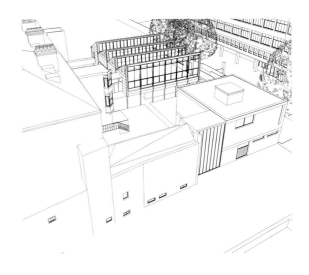

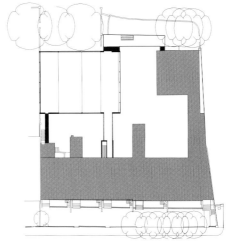

↖ | Window detail
↑↑ | 3D model
↑ | Floor plan
↙ | Exterior view
↓ | Sections

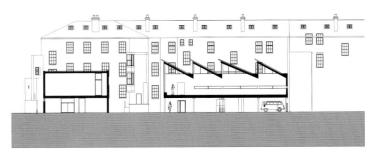

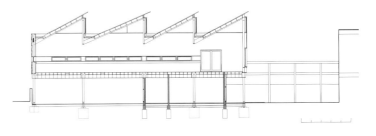

↑ | **View from north**
→ | **Library wing**

Faculty of Education
Cambridge

The project's design sets an interior social street, winding through the garden from entrance lawn on the east side to the gardens on the BDP west. Along the north side of the street is placed a library, which is depressed into the lawn along the edge of the trees to receive glare free north light. Along the south side flexible teaching, seminar rooms and office space form a structured back-drop to the high side of Homerton College. The form and materials reflect the uses, orientation and relationships with college and garden. The section cascades down from the structured brick box for learning, "the brick house", through the sinuous wooden structure of the library "the timber house".

PROJECT FACTS **Address:** 184 Hills Road, Cambridge CB2 8PQ, United Kingdom. **Client:** University of Cambridge. **Completion:** 2004. **Size:** 5,000 m².

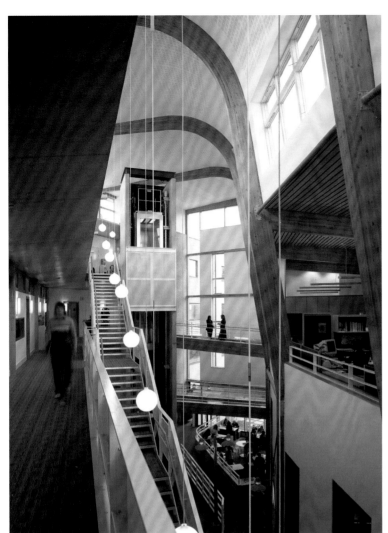

← | Galleries
↓ | Sections
↙ | Floor plans
→ | East entrance
↘ | Library interior

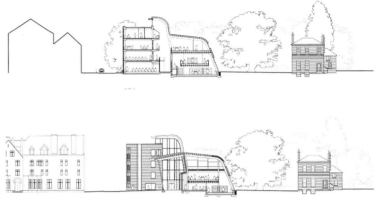

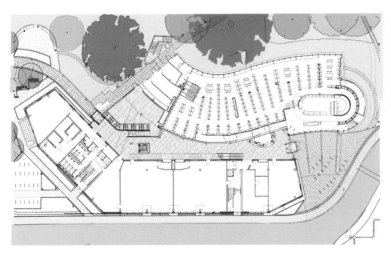

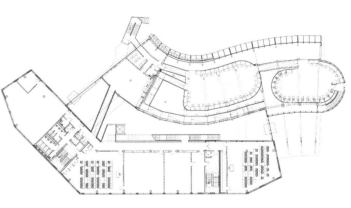

↑ | **Exterior view**
→ | **Façade**

Art & Design Academy

Liverpool

Merging the John Moores University's art and design faculties, the building's serpentine form bends and curves to reflect the shape of the site, aligning primarily with the base of the Metropolitan Catholic Cathedral. The sculptural form is emphasised by the splayed walls of the studios which provide shade from direct sunlight while maximising natural light from the north. Spanning three stories this entrance draws students, staff and visitors into the central atrium, the social heart of the building. The 11,000 square meters of floor space is distributed over six floors. The lower ground and ground floors provide shared facilities, including the Tate café, seminar rooms, a 350-seat multi-purpose space, galleries and exhibition spaces.

PROJECT FACTS

Address: 2 Duckinfield Street, Liverpool L3 5RD, United Kingdom. **Client:** Liverpool John Moores University. **Completion:** 2009. **Size:** 11,000 m².

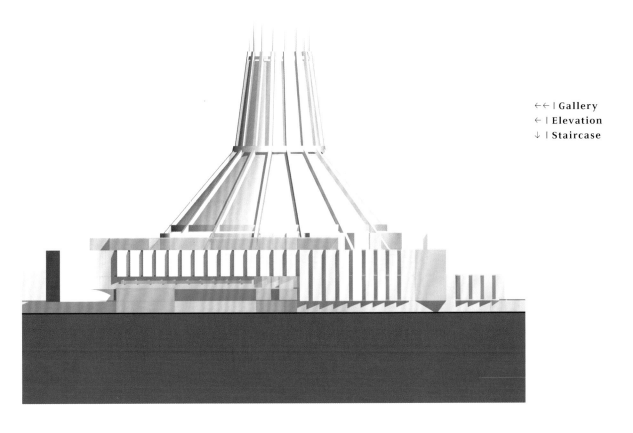

←← | Gallery
← | Elevation
↓ | Staircase

↑ | **Visualisation**
→ | **Construction site**

Campus Commons
New Paltz

The Campus Commons is a "crystalline palisade" set between the existing brutalist concrete student union building and the administration building at the campus entrance. The addition fills an existing open court set between the two existing buildings. The expressive form of the addition is influenced by the regional landscape of the Hudson River Valley where it is sited. The forms are drawn from the vistas of the Shawangunk ridge and create an exterior sculptural expression of the landscape and a dramatic interior commons. A structural stress skin system of exposed steel tubes creates a column-free interior space for gathering.

PROJECT FACTS
Address: 1 Hawk Drive, New Paltz, NY 12561–2443, United States of America. **Client:** The State University of New York at New Paltz. **Completion:** 2010. **Size:** 1,115 m².

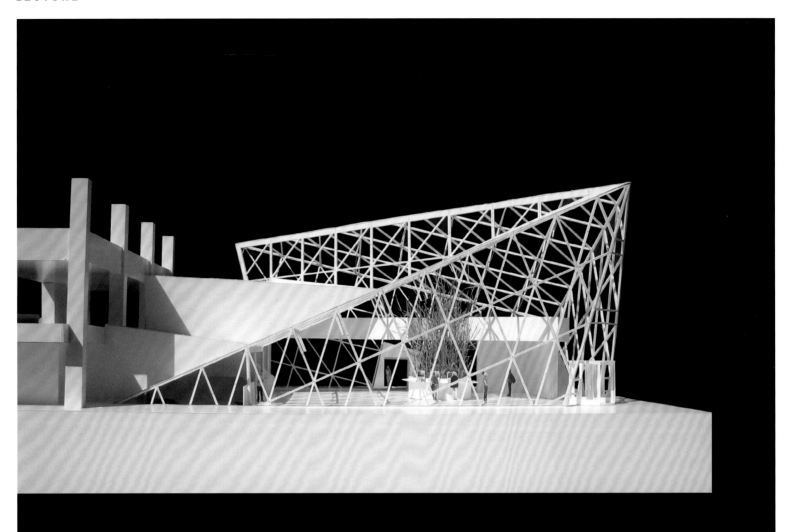

↖↖ | Model
←← | Visualisation
↑ | Construction site
← | Floor plans
↙ | Sketch
↓ | Site plan

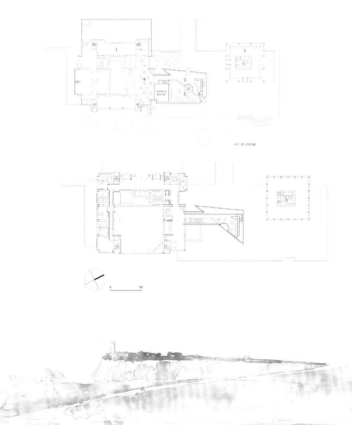

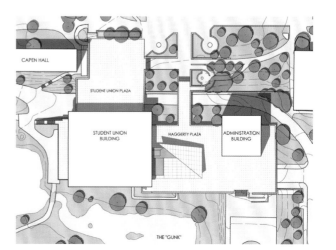

↑ | **Exterior view**
→ | **Façade**

Kilen

Frederiksberg

"Kilen" takes its shape and name from its long, wedge shaped geometry and consists of a sharp-cut prismatic four-story main body resting on an organically shaped one-story base which ties the building together with the surrounding landscape. The two equal-ranking entrances to the building take the form of passages through softly modelled grass mounds. The landscape is transported into the ground plan of the building, forming distinct amphi structures where the most outward-facing functions are placed – café, lounge and study places as well as access to conference facilities and large group rooms. The building interior is organised as a shell-shaped atrium which runs through all five stories as a unifying spatial focus. Daylight from lights in the roof plane is drawn through the atrium into the depth of the building.

PROJECT FACTS

Address: Kilevej 14, 2000 Frederiksberg, Denmark. **Client:** Copenhagen Business School. **Landscape architects:** Marianne Levinsen and Algren & Bruun. **Completion:** 2005. **Size** 10,700 m².

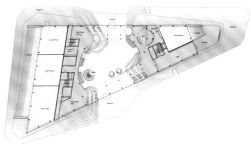

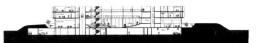

↖↖ | Atrium
← | Courtyard
↖ | Stairs
↑↑ | Site plan
↑ | Section

Davidsson Tarkela Architects,
Aki Davidsson and Hannele
Storgårds, architects SAFA

↑ | **Bird's eye view**
→ | **Yard,** detail

Aleksandria Learning Center

Helsinki

Aleksandria Learning Center is a part of the downtown campus of the University of Helsinki. It contains various facilities, such as individual and team work points for online studies, teaching and seminar facilities, the IT department, the teaching technology center and the language center. The new building is concealed in the center of the block. It is designed to cater for large numbers of users, providing an open learning environment for both university lecturers and students. Due to the nature of the activities an open building solution that would emphasise an interactive approach was sought after. Natural light is supplied through the adjacent open courtyard and a covered light well.

PROJECT FACTS
Address: Fabianinkatu 28, 00100 Helsinki, Finland. **Client:** University of Helsinki. **Completion:** 2003.
Size: 5,730 m².

↖ | **Basement corridor**
← | **Entrance area**
↓ | **Section**

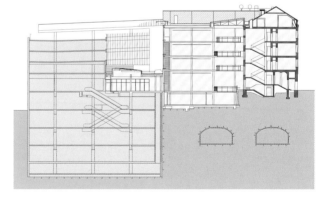

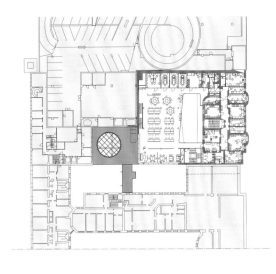

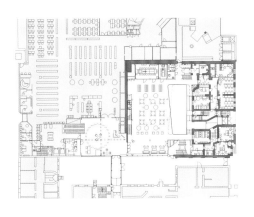

↖ | Lightwell
↑ | Floor plans
↙ | Exterior view

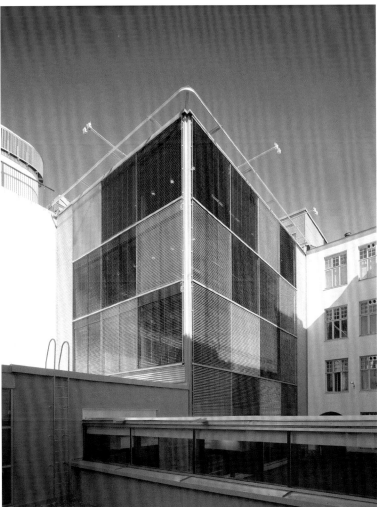

↑ | **External view**
→ | **Façade**

Exactum

Helsinki

"Exactum" was drawn up on the basis of an architectural competition in 2004. The building is part of the Helsinki University Kumpula campus area and a long-term plan in which laboratory, teaching and research facilities of various university departments are concentrated on three campuses outside the city center. The Department of Mathematics and Statistics, and the Department of Computer Science are in "Exactum". The main materials of the façades, whitened concrete block and an untreated aluminum grid, are repeated inside the building. The wood and veneer surfaces give color and warmth to the pedestrian routes.

PROJECT FACTS

Address: Gustaf Hällströmin katu 2b, 00014 Helsingin Yliopisto, Finland. **Client:** Senate Properties, University Premises, Helsinki University, Department of the Mathematics and Statistics, Department of Computer Science and the Department of Seismology. **Completion:** 2004. **Size:** 10,020 m².

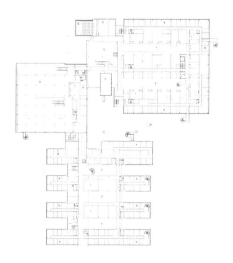

↖ | Atrium
↑ | Floor plans
← | Window
↓ | Sections
↗ | Stairs
→ | Lecture hall

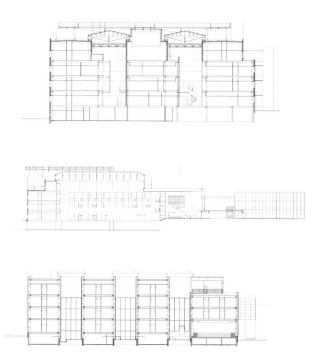

↑ | **Front view**
→ | **Façade**

Physicum

Helsinki

"Physicum" and "Exactum" were drawn up on the basis of an architectural competition. The buildings are part of the Helsinki University Kumpula campus area and a long-term plan in which laboratory, teaching and research facilities of various university departments are concentrated on three campuses outside the city center. The main concept was to develop functionally and architecturally dense units, which are grouped along a common external space. Taking into account the topography of the area – Kumpula hill is one of the highest spots in the city – the new campus will have an important role both symbolically and from a cityscape point of view. The facilities of the Department of Physical Sciences have been placed in "Physicum", as well as a library servicing the whole campus.

PROJECT FACTS **Address:** Väinö Auerinkatu 11, Helsinki, Finland. **Client:** Senate Properties, University Premises, Helsinki University, Department of Physical Sciences, Department of Geology, Department of Geography, Kumpula Science Library. **Completion:** 2001. **Size:** 16,737 m².

←← | Night shot
← | Entrance
↙↙ | Stairs
↙ | Cafeteria
↖ | Interior view
↓ | Lecture hall

↑ | Exterior view
→ | Interior view

Computer and Conference Center

London

The building consists of a 400-seat lecture theater, foyer and university entrance, general teaching rooms and a 400-screen computer library. The lecture theater on the first floor, which acts as an architectural pivot between the entrance road and the new College Green, is clad in fiber-cement and features two unique corner windows. The entrance foyer is located underneath it. A fire-escape doubles as a direct passage to a vomitorium entrance to the theater above (also useful for late-comers). However, the main entrances are the entrance to the teaching accommodations in the rear and an angled staircase with a direct view of the computer library on the first floor. Externally, a vaulted passage links the first College Green courtyard to the emerging second courtyard.

PROJECT FACTS

Address: University of East London, Stratford Campus, Romford Road, London E15 4LZ, United Kingdom. **Client:** University of East London. **Completion:** 2009. **Size:** 2,800 m².

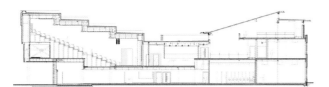

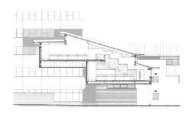

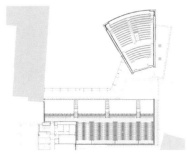

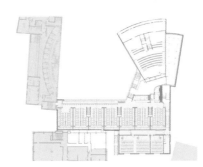

↖ | Sections
← | Floor plans
↓ | View towards lecture theater
↗ | View across new College Green
↘ | Computer center

Index

Arch

itects Index

ARCHITECTS INDEX

ANMA
Agence Nicolas Michelin & Associés
Nicolas Michelin – Michel Delplace –
Cyril Trétou

9, Cour des Petites Écuries
75010 Paris (France)
T +33 1 53 34 00 01
F +33 1 53 34 09 99
agence@anma.fr
www.anma.fr

→ 190

ATELIER DESHAUS

C3-202 Red Town
No. 570 West Huaihai Rd.
Shanghai 200052 (China)
T +86 21 61248118
F +86 21 61248119
info@deshaus.com
www.deshaus.com

→ 38, 42, 46

BDP

16 Brewhouse Yard
London EC1V 4LJ (United Kingdom)
T +44 20 7812 8000
F +44 20 7812 8399
enquiries@bdp.com
www.bdp.com

→ 232

du Besset-Lyon architects

30, rue Ligner
75020 Paris (France)
T +33 143 671 675
F +33 143 670 016
email@dubesset-lyon.com
www.dubesset-lyon.com

→ 24

Tilman Bock Norbert Sachs Architekten BDA

Knesebeckstraße 86/87
10623 Berlin (Germany)
T +49 30 23 62 00 01
F +49 30 23 62 00 19
info@bock-sachs-architekten.de
www.bock-sachs-architekten.de

→ 172

Broadway Malyan

Interchange Place
151-165 Edmund Street
Birmingham B3 2TA (United Kingdom)
T +44 121 236 2030
F +44 121 237 2080
hello@broadwaymalyan.com
www.broadwaymalyan.com

→ 120

CODE UNIQUE ARCHITEKTEN

Katharinenstraße 5
01099 Dresden (Germany)
T +49 351 810 788 00
F +49 351 810 788 25
contact@codeunique.de
www.codeunique.de

→ 28

Davidsson Tarkela Architects, Aki Davidsson and Hannele Storgårds, architects SAFA

Pälkäneentie 19 A
00510 Helsinki (Finland)
T +358 9 4342060
F +358 9 43420615
firstname.lastname@arkdt.fi
www.arkdt.fi

→ 248

Jeanne Dekkers Architectuur

Postbus 3001
2601 DA Delft (The Netherlands)
T +31 15 2152969
F +31 15 2152960
info@jeannedekkers.nl
www.jeannedekkers.nl

→ 92

Erick van Egeraat

Calandstraat 23
3016 CA Rotterdam (The Netherlands)
T +31 10 436 9686
F +31 10 436 9573
info@erickvanegeraat.com
www.erickvanegeraat.com

→ 50, 88

Ehrlich Architects

10865 Washington Boulevard
Culver City, CA 90232 (USA)
T +1 310 838 9700
F +1 310 838 9737
info@ehrlicharchitects.com
www.ehrlicharchitects.com

→ 162

DFA | Dietmar Feichtinger Architectes

11, rue des Vignoles
75020 Paris (France)
T +33 1 43 71 15 22
F +33 1 43 70 67 20
contact.paris@feichtingerarchitectes.com
www.feichtingerarchitectes.com

→ 62

Ernst Giselbrecht + Partner
architektur zt gmbh

Brockmanngasse 48
8010 Graz (Austria)
T +43 316 81 70 50
F +43 316 81 70 50 9
office@giselbrecht.at
www.giselbrecht.at

→ 156

Haworth Tompkins

19-20 Great Sutton Street
London EC1V 0DR (United Kingdom)
T +44 207 250 3225
F +44 207 250 3226
info@haworthtompkins.com
www.haworthtompkins.com

→ 152

HCP DESIGN AND PROJECT MANAGEMENT PVT LTD

Paritosh, Usmanpura
Ahmedabad 380 013 (India)
T +91 79 27550875
F +91 79 27552924
hcpahd@hcp.co.in
www.hcp.co.in

→ 216

Ferdinand Heide Architekt BDA

Leinwebergasse 4
60386 Frankfurt am Main (Germany)
T +49 69 420827 0
F +49 69 420827 29
info@ferdinand-heide.de
www.ferdinand-heide.de

→ 96

Steven Holl Architects

450 W. 31st street, 11th floor
New York, NY 10001 (USA)
T +1 212 629 7262
F +1 212 629 7312
nyc@stevenholl.com
www.stevenholl.com

→ 54, 220

Jean Marc Ibos Myrto Vitart architects

4, Cité Paradis
75010 Paris (France)
T +33 144838580
F +33 144838581
jmimv@ibosvitart.com
www.ibosvitart.com

→ 184

ikon.5 architects

864 Mapleton Road, Suite 100
Princeton, NJ 08540 (USA)
T +1 609 919 0099
F +1 609 919 0088
jtattoni@ikon5architects.com
www.ikon5architects.com

→ 114, 240

Jarmund/Vigsnæs
AS Architects MNAL

Hausmanns gate 6
0186 Oslo (Norway)
T +47 22 99 43 43
F +47 22 99 43 53
jva@jva.no
www.jva.no

→ 126

Joachim Kleine Allekotte Architekten

Köpenicker Straße 48/49, Aufgang F
10179 Berlin (Germany)
T +49 30 315185 00
F +49 30 315185 51
info@kleineallekotte-architekten.com
www.kleineallekotte-architekten.com

→ 144

KNOCHE ARCHITEKTEN BDA

Holbeinstraße 24
04229 Leipzig (Germany)
T +49 341 870 99 08 0
F +49 341 870 99 08 9
info@knoche-architekten.de
www.knoche-architekten.de

→ 166

Architects Lahdelma & Mahlamäki

Tehtaankatu 29 A
00150 Helsinki (Finland)
T +358 9 2511 020
F +358 9 2511 0210
firstname.surname@arklm.fi
www.arklm.fi

→ 252, 256

Henning Larsen Architects

Vesterbrogade 76
1620 Copenhagen V (Denmark)
T +45 8233 3000
F +45 8233 3099
mail@henninglarsen.com
www.henninglarsen.com

→ 18

LUNDGAARD & TRANBERG ARKITEKTER A/S

Pilestræde 10, 3. Sal
1112 Copenhagen (Denmark)
T +45 33 91 07 17
F +45 33 91 07 16
mail@ltarkitekter.dk
www.ltarkitekter.dk

→ 244

Lyons

Level 3, 246 Bourke Street
Melbourne, VIC 3000 (Australia)
T +613 9600 2818
F +613 9600 2819
lyons@lyonsarch.com.au
www.lyonsarch.com.au

→ 136

Rick Mather Architects

123 Camden High Street
London NW1 7JR (United Kingdom)
T +44 207 284 1727
F +44 207 267 7826
info@rickmather.com
www.rickmather.com

→ 208, 236

me di um Architekten
Roloff Ruffing und Partner

Oberstraße 14
20144 Hamburg (Germany)
T +49 40 420 50 24
F +49 40 420 90 98
office@medium-architekten.de
www.medium-architekten.de

→ 180

hg merz architekten museumsgestalter

Ostendstraße 110
70188 Stuttgart (Germany)
T +49 711 707128 0
F +49 711 707128 60
stuttgart@hgmerz.com
www.hgmerz.com

→ 212

MIRALLES TAGLIABUE EMBT

Passatge de la Pau 10 bis Pral
08002 Barcelona (Spain)
T +34 93 4125342
F +34 93 4123718
info@mirallestagliabue.com
www.mirallestagliaue.com

→ 68

MJP Architects

9 Heneage Street
Spitalfields, London E1 5LJ (United Kingdom)
T +44 20 7377 9262
F +44 20 7247 7854
mail@mjparchitects.co.uk
www.mjparchitects.co.uk

→ 110

MOLE Architects

The Black House, Kingdon Avenue
Prickwillow, Ely
Cambridge, Cambridgeshire, CB7 4UL (United Kingdom)
T +44 13 53 688 287
F +44 13 53 688 287
studio@molearchitects.co.uk
www.molearchitects.co.uk

→ 228

Arkitektfirmaet C. F. Møller A/S

Europaplads 2, 11th floor
8000 Aarhus C (Denmark)
T +45 8730 5300
F +45 8730 5399
cfmoller@cfmoller.com
www.cfmoller.com

→ 80, 84, 224

Richard Murphy Architects

15 Old Fishmarket Close
Edinburgh EH1 1RW (United Kingdom)
T +44 131 220 6124
F +44 131 220 6781
mail@richardmurphyarchitects.com
www.richardmurphyarchitects.com

→ 140, 200, 260

Périphériques architects

4, Passage de la Fonderie
75011 Paris (France)
T +33 1 43 55 59 95
F I33 1 43 55 64 84
agences@peripheriques-architectes.com
www.peripheriques-architectes.com

→ 32

Dominique Perrault Architecture

6, rue Bouvier
75011 Paris (France)
T +33 1 44 06 00 00
F +33 1 44 06 00 01
dpa@d-p-a.fr
www.perraultarchitecte.com

→ 12

RMJM

500 Alexander Park
Princeton, NJ 08543 (USA)
T +1 609 452 8888
F +1 609 452 8839
princeton@rmjm.com
www.rmjm.com

→ 76, 106, 204

Saucier + Perrotte architectes

7043 Waverly
Montreal, QB H25 3J1 (Canada)
T +1 514 273 1700
F +1 514 273 3501
contact_spa@saucierperrotte.com
www.saucierperrotte.com

→ 56, 176

Seung H-Sang

2-8 Dongsung-dong, Jongro-gu
Seoul (Korea)
T +52 82 2 763 2010
F +52 82 2 745 3606
master@iroje.com
www.iroje.com

→ 72

schmidt hammer lassen architects

Aaboulevarden 37, PO box 5117
8000 Aarhus C (Denmark)
T +45 86 20 19 00
F +45 86 18 45 13
info@shl.dk
www.shl.dk

→ 102

schulz & schulz

Lampestraße 6
04107 Leipzig (Germany)
T +49 341 487133
F +49 341 4871345
schulz@schulzarchitekten.de
www.schulzarchitekten.de

→ **132**

Tham & Videgård Arkitekter

Blekingegatan 46
11662 Stockholm (Sweden)
T +46 8 7020046
F +46 8 7020056
info@tvark.se
www.tvark.se

→ **196**

ZHANG LEI / AZL architects

1517-15th floor, FeiYiMin Building, Nanjing University
Nanjing 210093 (China)
T +86 25 51861369
F +86 25 51861367
atelierzhanglei@163.com
www.AZLarchitects.com

→ **148**

AZL architects — 148–151
Bakker, Marco — 50, 88 (portrait)
Baril, Pol — 178 b.
Binet, Helene, London — 153, 154 a.
Boegly, Luc — 32–37
Broadway Malyan — 120–123
Butler, David, London — 228–230, 231 b.
Chalmeau, Stéphane — 190–193
Chivers, Richard — 236–239
Cook, Peter, London — 230 a.
Cramer, Marc — 56–61, 176, 177, 178 a., 179
Dale, Nils Petter — 126–131
Eskerod, Torben — 80, 82
Feichtinger, Barbara — 62, 64–67
Fessy, Georges, Lyon — 184–186, 188 a., 189
Frahm, Klaus — 180–183
Gascoigne, Chris, Edinburgh — 106, 107, 109
Gaultier, Alex — 68–71
John Golling Photography — 136, 137, 138 a., 139 a.
Hamilton Knight, Martine, UK — 232–235
HCPDPM, Ahmedabad — 216–219
Heinen, Frank — 96, 100
Heinz, Volkmar — 89, 90
Heitoff, Mark — 54, 220 (portrait)
Henriksen, Poul Ib, Denmark — 224–227
Hufton & Crow, London — 204–207
Hunter, Keith, Edinburgh — 108
ikon.5 architects, Princeton — 114–117, 240–243
Jorgensen, Tom — 54, 55
Kida, Katsuhisa, Fototeca, Japan — 154 b.
Kim, Dong-Yul — 72 (portrait)
Ling, Bobo – Fotolia.com — 10/11
Matthews, Andy, Rick Mather Architects — 208–211
Meinel, Udo, Berlin — 212–215
MEW — 80, 84, 224 (portraits)
C. F. Møller, Denmark — 84–87
Morin, André / DPA / Adagp — 12–17
Morin, Eric — 68 (portrait)
Mork, Adam — 18–23
Müller-Naumann, Stefan, Munich — 132–135
Müller, Stefan, Berlin — 144–147
Murai, Osamu — 72–75
Niemelä, Voitto — 254 b.
Nisonen, Pertti — 258 a.

Ott, Paul — 156–159
Richard Murphy Architects — 140–143, 200–203, 260–263
Olsen, Erik W. — 81
Perrault Projets, Adagp — 12–17
Pilipipa – Fotolia.com — 124/125
Richters, Christian — 50–53
RMJM — 76–79
Ruault, Philippe, Paris — 187, 188 b.
Ryan, Andy — 220–223
Scagliola, Daria, Rotterdam — 92–95
Schmitt, Christian — 97
Smith MD, Carolina K. – Fotolia.com — 170/171
Dianna Snape Photography — 138 b., 139 b.
Spiluttini, Margherita, Vienna — 63
Staubach, Barbara, Frankfurt — 98
Sumesgutner, Daniel, Hamburg — 190–193
Tiainen, Jussi, Helsinki — 248–254 a., 255–257, 258 b., 259
Tham & Videgaard Arkitekter, Stockholm — 196–199
Timmerman, Bill — 162–165
Träupmann, Dietmar, Augustusburg — 166–169
Vile, Philip, Aarhus — 102–105
Vile, Philip, London — 152, 155
Vinken, Frank, Essen — 212 (portrait)
Waahlström, Erik, Stockholm — 196 (portrait)
van Wendel, de Joode Ries, Dordrecht — 92 (portrait)
Winther, Jan Kofod — 83
Wuthenow, Hans Joachim, Berlin — 96 b.
Yichun, Liu, Shanghai — 42–45, 50, 53
Zenke, Yvonne — 88
Zhangsiye, Shanghai — 46–49, 51, 52

All other pictures were made available by the architects.

Cover front: LUNDGAARD & TRANBERG ARKITEKTER (Kilen by LUNDGAARD & TRANBERG ARKITEKTER)
Cover back: left: Tilman Bock, Norbert Sachs (Lecture Hall in Zittau by Tilman Bock, Norbert Sachs)
right: LUNDGAARD & TRANBERG ARKITEKTER (Kilen by LUNDGAARD & TRANBERG ARKITEKTER)

IMPRINT

The Deutsche Nationalbibliothek lists this publication in
the Deutsche Nationalbibliografie; detailed bibliographical
data are available on the internet at http://dnb.d-nb.de.

//

ISBN 978-3-03768-036-0

//

© 2010 by Braun Publishing
www.braun-publishing.ch

//

//

1st edition 2010

//

Selection of projects: Sibylle Kramer
Project coordination: Marc von Reth
Translation: Cosima Talhouni
Graphic concept: ON Grafik | Tom Wibberenz
Layout: Marc von Reth

//